MATTHEW THROUGH ACTS

THEOLOGY OF WORK BIBLE COMMENTARY

MATTHEW THROUGH ACTS
VOLUME 4

THEOLOGY OF WORK PROJECT

HENDRICKSON PUBLISHERS

THEOLOGY OF WORK BIBLE COMMENTARY, VOLUME 4: MATTHEW THROUGH ACTS

ISBN 978-1-61970-526-5

Printed in the United States of America

First Printing — October 2014

Library of Congress Cataloging-in-Publication Data

Theology of work Bible commentary / by the Theology of Work Project ;
   Will Messenger, executive editor.
      volumes cm
   Includes bibliographical references and index.
      Contents: volume 4. Matthew through Acts — 1. Work—Religious aspects—
   Christianity. 2. Work—Biblical teaching. I. Messenger, Will, 1952- editor.
   II. Theology of Work Project (Hampton, Mass.)
      BT738.5.T45 2014
      220.8'331—dc23
                        2014022025

Table of Contents

Abbreviations

Old Testament

Gen.	Genesis	Eccl.	Ecclesiastes
Exod.	Exodus	Song	Song of Songs
Lev.	Leviticus	Isa.	Isaiah
Num.	Numbers	Jer.	Jeremiah
Deut.	Deuteronomy	Lam.	Lamentations
Josh.	Joshua	Ezek.	Ezekiel
Judg.	Judges	Dan.	Daniel
Ruth	Ruth	Hos.	Hosea
1 Sam.	1 Samuel	Joel	Joel
2 Sam.	2 Samuel	Amos	Amos
1 Kgs.	1 Kings	Obad.	Obadiah
2 Kgs.	2 Kings	Jonah	Jonah
1 Chr.	1 Chronicles	Mic.	Micah
2 Chr.	2 Chronicles	Nah.	Nahum
Ezra	Ezra	Hab.	Habakkuk
Neh.	Nehemiah	Zeph.	Zephaniah
Est.	Esther	Hag.	Haggai
Job	Job	Zech.	Zechariah
Ps(s).	Psalm(s)	Mal.	Malachi
Prov.	Proverbs		

New Testament

Matt.	Matthew	Rom.	Romans
Mark	Mark	1 Cor.	1 Corinthians
Luke	Luke	2 Cor.	2 Corinthians
John	John	Gal.	Galatians
Acts	Acts	Eph.	Ephesians

Phil.	Philippians	James	James
Col.	Colossians	1 Pet.	1 Peter
1 Thess.	1 Thessalonians	2 Pet.	2 Peter
2 Thess.	2 Thessalonians	1 John	1 John
1 Tim.	1 Timothy	2 John	2 John
2 Tim.	2 Timothy	3 John	3 John
Titus	Titus	Jude	Jude
Philem.	Philemon	Rev.	Revelation
Heb.	Hebrews		

Any commentary references not in this particular volume can be found at the Theology of Work website (www.theologyofwork.org), along with video interviews and sidebars on people in the work world.

Foreword

The *Theology of Work Bible Commentary* is unique in that it explores what the entire Bible says about work. It represents more than five years of research by 140 contributors from sixteen countries, guided by an international steering committee of twenty scholars, pastors, and Christians from a variety of workplaces. We are thankful to God for this opportunity to present it to you in this volume.

Why does anyone need a theology of work? When we talk about a "theology," it can sound as stuffy as a tomb. Theology is often considered the domain of scholars who are wrestling with questions that no one ever asks, or solving problems that have never really arisen. When we talk about theology, however, we are really talking about what we know or do not know about God. Everyone does theology. Atheists who say they don't believe in God are already dealing with theology. Wars are fought over theology by people who are convinced that they are doing God's will. Agree with them or not, everyone everywhere does theology. People in the workplace who may never attend church are dealing with theology in some way every day. Ultimately, the questions we ask about God are not merely religious, they are life altering. In fact, what you believe about God may be the most important thing you ever think about. That's theology!

When it comes to work, theology is seldom practiced out loud. During my early years as president at Denver Seminary, I hosted a morning Bible study for business people. After class, over breakfast, we discussed the myriad dilemmas these workers and leaders faced in the workplace. Again and again, I heard, "You're the first pastoral person to actively address how my faith relates to my work." It was then that I realized there was a great divide between the leadership of the church and the everyday lives of the people they are called to equip.

At its heart, the perceived distance between God and everyday work is a theological issue. Most Christians believe that God cares about how we relate to others, how we relate to him, and whether we cheat, steal, lie, or break the Ten Commandments. However, it would surprise a lot of us to learn that our work matters to God. God cares what we do for a living, how we do it, and how we use our resources. As it turns out, the Bible has much to say about work. In fact, work is a major topic in the Bible, beginning with the surprising statement in Genesis 2:15 that God created people to work—not as a punishment, but as a pleasure and a way of relating to God himself.

The Scriptures provide principles that both give *meaning* to work and tell us *how* to work. Unfortunately, there is not a book in the Bible called First and Second Executive or Letter to the Christian Plumbers. Instead, what the Bible teaches about God's view of work is embedded in the Scriptures. Only a few of the biblical writers speak directly about the work that people do. They simply assume it. For instance, one of the Ten Commandments declares, "Remember the sabbath day and keep it holy" (Exod. 20:8), as if the only day God cared about was the Sabbath. But the command also says, "Six days you shall labor and do all your work" (Exod. 20:9). So the command deals not only with a special day when we can rest, but with the other days of the week designed for work.

The *Theology of Work Bible Commentary* goes through the Bible book by book to bring to the surface what we might not have seen about work at first blush. For example, consider the last book of the Bible, Revelation. It is possible to be so caught up in the visions in Revelation and questions about when they will occur, that we do not see that the Scripture also tells us about work now and in the future. You might be surprised that the Song of Solomon, a love poem, has quite a bit to say about workers and work. This book attempts through a study of the Scriptures to answer the question, "Does the work we do matter to God?"

This commentary deals with the theology of *work*. In that sense, it is limited. And in another sense, it is very broad. It is limited to work, but work is as diverse as are the people in the world. One question that may come to mind is, "What is work?" The answer to that question seems obvious. Work is what we do to make a living. Saying that, however, implies that people work for forty or fifty hours a week in order to live for the other hours of the week. There is more to work than that. A farmer, for example, doesn't "work to make a living." Plowing a field, planting a crop, bringing in a harvest is really his life. Or when we say that people "work to make a living," we imply that they work to receive a salary or a wage. But what about volunteers who travel to another country at their own expense to help people who have suffered in an earthquake or a flood? What about the person who raises children, cooks meals, and takes care of the family home? Certainly these people work, and work hard, but do not receive a salary. What, then, do we mean when we talk about their "work"?

Others might insist that the opposite of work is play. These are the folks who say, "TGIF: Thank God, it's Friday and the weekend is coming!" The recreation we enjoy on the weekend stands in contrast to the labor we put in during the week. But what about the professional basketball or tennis player? Do they work? How does their "work" differ from recreation?

If you own a business, what responsibility do you have to the people who work for you and to the people who buy your products or services? If you're an employee, does God care about the products you make or the way your company advertises them? Is what you talk about when you're having coffee with co-workers important to God? Does God have anything to do with the work that consumes a major part of your life?

If you're a pastor reading this material on a theology of work, do you find yourself thinking about a woman in the eighth row, three seats from the end, who works in financial services, or the man behind her who is a nurse? Or a couple on the other side of the sanctuary who has recently invested everything they have to open a restaurant? Do you think about yourself as a pastor? Do you work? Perhaps you are tempted to respond, "Of course I do, but it's really not the same thing. I have a special calling from God." That leads to another question: What do you mean by a "call"? Is it reserved for missionaries, teachers at a Bible college or a seminary, or translators of the Bible? How about the executive, the vice president of an insurance company, or the bus driver who attends your church? Do they have a call from God? Does God call men and women in business, government, or nonprofit organizations to their positions? Can you imagine God "calling" a pastor to go back into the world of work? Is that whole way of thinking true to the Bible?

So you see, there is a flood of questions about the simple concept of work. In fact, we are barraged by questions about work that have to be answered. This commentary will not answer these sticky issues by providing a set of rules, but it will give you direction in coming to your own conclusions. After all, the Scriptures resemble a compass rather than a road map. But when you're on the journey, a compass can be very helpful. The *Theology of Work Bible Commentary* helps us plumb the depths of God's word, so that we can hear and respond to Jesus' voice in the calling of our everyday work.

Haddon W. Robinson
President
Theology of Work Project

Harold John Ockenga Distinguished Professor of Preaching
Gordon-Conwell Theological Seminary
Hamilton, Massachusetts, USA

Introduction to the Theology of Work

Work is not only a human calling, but also a divine one. "In the beginning God created the heavens and the earth." God worked to create us and created us to work. "The LORD God took the man and put him in the garden of Eden to till it and keep it" (Gen. 2:15). God also created work to be good, even if it's hard to see in a fallen world. To this day, God calls us to work to support ourselves and to serve others (Eph. 4:28).

Work can accomplish many of God's purposes for our lives—the basic necessities of food and shelter, as well as a sense of fulfillment and joy. Our work can create ways to help people thrive; it can discover the depths of God's creation; and it can bring us into wonderful relationships with co-workers and those who benefit from our work (customers, clients, patients, and so forth).

Yet many people face drudgery, boredom, or exploitation at work. We have bad bosses, hostile relationships, and unfriendly work environments. Our work seems useless, unappreciated, faulty, frustrating. We don't get paid enough. We get stuck in dead-end jobs or laid off or fired. We fail. Our skills become obsolete. It's a struggle just to make ends meet. But how can this be if God created work to be good—and what can we do about it? God's answers for these questions must be somewhere in the Bible, but where?

The Theology of Work Project's mission has been to study what the Bible says about work and to develop resources to apply the Christian faith to our work. It turns out that every book of the Bible gives practical, relevant guidance that can help us do our jobs better, improve our relationships at work, support ourselves, serve others more effectively, and find meaning and value in our work. The Bible shows us how to live all of life—including work—in Christ. Only in Jesus can we and our work be transformed to become the blessing it was always meant to be.

To put it another way, if we are not following Christ during the 100,000 hours of our lives that we spend at work, are we really following Christ? Our lives are more than just one day a week at church. The fact is that God cares about our life *every day of the week*. But how do we become equipped to follow Jesus at work? In the same ways we become equipped for every aspect of life in Christ—listening to sermons, modeling our lives on others' examples, praying for God's guidance, and most of all by studying the Bible and putting it into practice.

This Theology of Work series contains a variety of books to help you apply the Scriptures and Christian faith to your work. This book is one volume in the multivolume *Theology of Work Bible Commentary*, examining what the Gospels and the book of Acts say about work. These commentaries are intended to assist those with theological training or interest to conduct in-depth research into passages or books of Scripture.

Pastors will find these volumes helpful as they consider the Bible's perspective on work when teaching on particular passages or topics. Professors may use the commentary to help prepare classes or as a textbook for students. Laypeople may find practical help for workplace decisions (the topical index could be helpful in this regard), or they may read it as part of their personal or group Bible study. Other books in the Theology of Work series include Bible studies adapted from the *Theology of Work Commentary* and additional materials to help apply the Christian faith to daily work.

Christians today recognize God's calling to us in and through our work—for ourselves and for those whom we serve. May God use this book to help you follow Christ in every sphere of life and work.

Will Messenger, Executive Editor
Theology of Work Project

MATTHEW AND WORK

Introduction to Matthew

Work is an essential component of God's kingdom. Matthew, the tax-collector-turned-apostle, recounts Jesus' actions and teachings to show us how God intends us to live and work in his new kingdom. As followers of Jesus Christ, we live in two worlds. We stand with one foot in the human world, where our work may be subject to unspoken expectations that may or may not be in accordance with God's ways. At the same time, as Christians, we are subjects of God's kingdom, committed to his values and expectations. In telling the story of Jesus, Matthew shows us how to navigate the human world using God's compass. In doing so, he constantly points us toward the world's true identity as the "kingdom of heaven." (Matthew uses "kingdom of heaven" and "kingdom of God" interchangeably; see Matt. 19:23–24). This kingdom "has come" to earth, even though it has not yet become completely realized here. Until it comes to completion, Jesus' followers are to live and work according to God's call as "resident aliens"[1] in this present world.

To guide us in this way of life and work, Jesus discusses workplace matters such as leadership and authority, power and influence, fair and unfair business practices, truth and deception, treatment of workers, conflict resolution, wealth and the necessities of life, workplace relationships, investing and saving, rest, and working in organizations with policies and practices that are at odds with biblical norms.

The Kingdom of Heaven Has Come Near

At the beginning of his earthly ministry, Jesus announces that "the kingdom of heaven has come near" (Matt. 4:17). When we read "kingdom

---

[1] Stanley Hauerwas and William Willimon, *Resident Aliens: Life in the Christian Colony* (Nashville: Abingdon Press, 1989).

of heaven," we may think of harps, clouds, and angel choirs, but Jesus is clear that the kingdom of heaven refers to God's rule on earth. The kingdom of heaven "*has come near.*" It has come *here* to *this* world.

The workplace consequences of living in God's kingdom are profound. Kingdoms are concerned with governance, economics, agriculture, production, justice, defense—issues we see in most workplaces. Jesus' teachings, as recorded by Matthew, speak directly to our life at work. In the Sermon on the Mount, he inducts his followers into the values, ethics, and practices of this new kingdom. In the Lord's Prayer, he instructs them to pray, "Your kingdom come. Your will be done, *on earth as it is in heaven*" (Matt. 6:9–10). The Gospel of Matthew concludes as Jesus commissions his followers to go to work throughout the world, because he has received "all authority in heaven and *on earth*" and will be present with them in their work on earth (Matt. 28:18–20). Matthew is clear that this kingdom is not fully realized on earth as we know it, but will reach completion when we see "the Son of Man coming on the clouds of heaven with power and great glory" (Matt. 24:30). Meanwhile, we turn our backs on the old ways of work, so that the new way of the kingdom of heaven is made visible in us as we live. Even now, we work according to its values and practices.

Working as Citizens of God's Kingdom (Matthew 1–4)

We live in what theologians call "the already, but not yet." The kingdom of heaven has already been inaugurated by Jesus in his earthly ministry, but has not yet been fully realized—not until Christ returns in person as King. Meanwhile, our lives—including our work, our leisure, our worship, our joy, and our sorrow—are framed by the reality of living in a world still subjected to the old, corrupt ways of the Fall (Gen. 3), yet claimed by its true Lord, Christ. As Christians, we put ourselves wholly under Jesus as Lord. Our habits on earth are now to reflect the coming kingdom of heaven. This is not to boast that we are more godly than others, but to accept the challenge of growing into God's ways. God calls his people to many different roles and occupations on earth. In all these roles and occupations, we are to live out the true reality: the reign of God that is coming from heaven to earth.

At the same time, we cannot escape the ills of the world brought on by the Fall, including death (1 Cor. 15:15–26), sin (John 1:29), and Satan (Rev. 12:9). Jesus himself experienced terrible, though temporary, suffering at the hands of sinful men, and so may we. In our work, we may suffer greatly through forced labor, permanent unemployment, or even work-related death. Or we may suffer in smaller ways as we deal with challenging co-workers, unpleasant working conditions, promotions deserved but not received, or a thousand other setbacks. Sometimes we suffer from the consequences of our own sin at work. Others may suffer much more than we, but all of us can learn from the Gospel of Matthew how to live as Christ-followers in a fallen world.

Why Should We Listen to Jesus? (Matthew 1–2)

The opening chapters of Matthew's Gospel narrate in rapid-fire succession stories demonstrating that Jesus is the Lord whose coming inaugurates the kingdom of heaven on earth. They explain who Jesus is in terms of Scripture fulfilled (the Messiah) and show that his entrance into the world is the epicenter of all of God's dealings with humanity. The Gospel of Matthew begins with a description of Jesus' ancestry and birth: the baby in a Bethlehem manger is in the line of Israel's great king, David, and is a true Hebrew, going back to Abraham (Matt. 1:1–2:23). With each story, Matthew's references to the Old Testament Scriptures show how Jesus' coming reflects a particular ancient text.[2] We listen to Jesus because he is God's anointed, the promised Messiah, God entering the world in human flesh (John 1:14).

Jesus Calling (Matthew 3–4)

Nearly thirty years have elapsed between chapters 2 and 3. John the Baptist reveals Jesus' true identity as the Son of God to the crowds

---

[2] For example, Matthew 1:18–25 refers to Isaiah 7:14; Matthew 2:1–6 to Micah 5:1–3, 2 Samuel 5:3, and 1 Chronicles 11:2; and Matthew 2:13–15 to Hosea 11:1.

at the Jordan River (Matt. 3:17). Then Jesus, following his baptism by John, successfully withstands the temptations of the devil in the wilderness (Matt. 4:1–11), in contrast to Adam or the Israelites who had failed. (For more about the temptations of Jesus, see "Luke 4:1–13" below in "Luke and Work.") In this, we preview the ancient roots of the coming kingdom: it is "Israel" as God originally intended it. And we see its revolutionary aspects; it brings victory over the prince of the fallen world.

Work is an essential element of God's intent for the world. When God created Adam, he immediately gave him work to do (Gen. 2:15); throughout the Old Testament, God's people were also given work to do (Exod. 20:9). It should not surprise us that Jesus, too, was a laborer (Matt. 13:55). Jesus' baptism, his wilderness temptations, and his prior work experience as a carpenter prepared him for the public work he would now begin (Matt. 4:12).

Here we encounter the first passage speaking directly to the question of calling. Soon after Jesus begins to preach the coming of the kingdom of heaven, he calls the first four of his disciples to follow him (Matt. 4:18–21). Others later respond to his call, making up the Twelve—the band of those called apart by Jesus to serve as his intimate students and the first servant-leaders for the renewed people of God (cf. Matt. 10:1–4; 19:28; Eph. 2:19–21). Each of the Twelve is required to leave his former occupation, income, and relationships in order to travel with Jesus throughout Galilee. (The personal, family, and social sacrifices this required are discussed under "Mark 1:16–20" in "Mark and Work.") To these and other followers, Jesus holds out no hope of security or family ties. When Jesus later calls the tax collector Matthew, the implication is that Matthew will give up his work of tax collecting (Matt. 9:9).[3]

Does a call from Jesus mean that we have to stop working at our current job and become a preacher, pastor, or missionary? Is this passage

---

[3] We see the same call to a radical life change in Jesus' injunction to a potential disciple: "Let the dead bury their own dead" (Matt. 8:18–22). As R. T. France put it, "The kingdom of heaven apparently involves a degree of fanaticism which is willing to disrupt the normal rhythms of social life." R. T. France, *The Gospel of Matthew*, New International Commentary on the New Testament (Grand Rapids: Eerdmans, 2007), 331.

teaching us that discipleship means abandoning nets and boats, saws and chisels, payrolls and profits?

The answer is no. This passage *describes* what happened to four men by the Sea of Galilee that day. But it does not *prescribe* the same thing for every follower of Jesus Christ. For the Twelve, following Jesus did mean leaving their professions and their families in order to itinerate with their roving master. Both then and now, there are professions that require similar sacrifices, including military service, sea trade, or diplomacy, among many others. At the same time, we know that even during Jesus' earthly ministry not all true believers in him quit their day jobs to follow him. He had many followers who remained in their homes and occupations. Often he made use of their ability to provide meals, lodging, and financial support for him and his companions (e.g., Simon the Leper in Mark 14:3, or Mary, Martha, and Lazarus in Luke 10:38, John 12:1–2). Often, they gave him entry to their local communities, which is something his traveling companions could not have done. Interestingly, Zacchaeus was also a tax collector (Luke 19:1–10), and although his life as a tax collector was transformed by Jesus, we see no evidence that he was called to leave the profession.

But this passage also leads us to a deeper truth about our work and following Christ. We may not have to give up our jobs, but we have to give up allegiance to ourselves, or to anyone or any system contrary to God's purposes. In a sense, we become double agents for God's kingdom. We may remain in our workplace. We may perform the same tasks. But now we employ our work to serve the new kingdom and our new master. We still work to bring home a paycheck, but at a deeper level we also work to serve people, as our master did. When you serve people because of your allegiance to Christ, "you serve the Lord Christ," as Paul puts it (Col. 3:24).

This is more radical than it may first appear. We are challenged in the work we do. To the extent possible, we should seek to do those things that bring human flourishing, either through our part in carrying on the creation mandate, or our part in carrying out the redemption mandate. In short, we do those things that support people's dreams and bring healing to the brokenness around us.

So we see that although a call from Jesus may not change *what* we do for a living, it always changes *why* we work. As followers of Jesus, we work above all to serve him. In turn, this leads to a change in *how* we work, and especially how we treat other people. The ways of the new King include compassion, justice, truth, and mercy; the ways of the old prince of this world are devastation, apathy, oppression, deceit, and vindictiveness. The latter can no longer have any role in our work. This is more challenging than it may appear, and we could never hope to do so on our own. The practices required to live and work in these new ways can arise only from God's power or blessing in our work, as will emerge in chapters 5 through 7.

The Kingdom of Heaven at Work in Us (Matthew 5–7)

Chapters 5 through 7 in Matthew's Gospel give us the most complete version of Jesus' Sermon on the Mount. While this very long passage (111 verses) is often treated as a series of discrete segments (thought by some to have been compiled from different teaching occasions), there is a cohesion and a flow of thought in the sermon that deepens our understanding of how the kingdom of heaven is at work in us, in our work, and in our family and community life.

The Beatitudes (Matthew 5:1–12)

The Sermon on the Mount opens with the beatitudes—eight statements beginning with the word *blessed*.[4] This word affirms a state of blessing that already exists. Each beatitude declares that a group of people usually regarded as afflicted is actually blessed. Those blessed do not have to do anything to attain this blessing. Jesus simply declares that they have already been blessed. Thus the beatitudes are first of all declarations of God's grace. They are not conditions of salvation or road maps to earn entry to God's kingdom.

---

[4] The word *blessed* translates the Greek word *makarios*. It doesn't pray for a blessing but affirms an existing state of blessedness. There is another Greek word, *eulogia*, which is also translated into English as "blessed." It is the word used to pray that God will bless or bring something good to a person or a community. It does not appear in the beatitudes.

Those who belong to each blessed group experience God's grace because the kingdom of heaven has come near. Consider the second beatitude, "Blessed are those who mourn" (Matt. 5:4). People do not normally think of mourning as a blessing. It is a sorrow. But with the coming of the kingdom of heaven, mourning becomes a blessing because the mourners "will be comforted." The implication is that God himself will do the comforting. The affliction of mourning becomes the blessing of profound relationship with God. That is a blessing indeed!

Although the primary purpose of the beatitudes is to declare the blessings given by God's kingdom, most scholars also regard them as painting a picture of the character of that kingdom.[5] As we step into God's kingdom, we hope to become more like those named as blessed— more meek, more merciful, more hungry for righteousness, more apt to make peace, and so on. This gives the beatitudes a moral imperative. Later, when Jesus says, "Make disciples of all nations" (Matt. 28:19), the beatitudes describe the character these disciples are meant to take on.

The beatitudes describe the character of God's kingdom, but they are not *conditions* of salvation. Jesus does not say, for example, "Only the pure in heart may enter the kingdom of heaven." This is good news because the beatitudes are impossibly hard to fulfill. Given that Jesus says, "Everyone who looks at a woman with lust has already committed adultery with her in his heart" (Matt. 5:28), who could truly be "pure in heart" (Matt. 5:8)? If it were not for God's grace, no one would actually be blessed. The beatitudes are not a judgment against all who fail to measure up. Instead, they are a blessing for any who consent to join themselves to God's kingdom as it "comes near."

A further grace of the beatitudes is that they bless God's community, not just God's individuals. By following Jesus, we become blessed members of the kingdom community, even though our character is not yet formed in God's likeness. Individually, we fail to fulfill the characteristics of some or all of the blessings. But we are blessed nonetheless by

---

[5] Donald A. Hagner, *Matthew 1–13*, vol. 33A, *Word Biblical Commentary* (Nashville: Thomas Nelson, 1993), 97. This view, though widely held, is not universal. For a brief outline of various alternatives, see W. F. Albright and C. S. Mann, *Matthew*, vol. 26 of *The Anchor Bible* (New York: Doubleday, 1971), 50–53.

the character of the entire community around us. Citizenship in God's kingdom begins now. The character of the kingdom community is perfected when Jesus returns, "coming on the clouds of heaven with power and great glory" (Matt. 24:30).

With this understanding, we are ready to examine the specific character of each of the beatitudes and explore how it applies to work. We cannot attempt to discuss each beatitude exhaustively, but we hope we can lay the groundwork for receiving the blessings and living out the beatitudes in our daily work.[6]

"Blessed Are the Poor in Spirit, for Theirs Is the Kingdom of Heaven" (Matthew 5:3)

The "poor in spirit" are those who cast themselves on God's grace.[7] We personally acknowledge our spiritual bankruptcy before God. It is the tax collector in the temple, beating his breast and saying, "God, be merciful to me, a sinner" (Luke 18:9–14). It is an honest confession that we are sinful and utterly without the moral virtues needed to please God. It is the opposite of arrogance. In its deepest form, it acknowledges our desperate need for God. Jesus is declaring that it is a blessing to recognize our need to be filled by God's grace.

Thus, at the very beginning of the Sermon on the Mount, we learn that we don't have the spiritual resources in ourselves to put Jesus' teachings into practice. We can't fulfill God's call by ourselves. Blessed

---

[6] For a deeper exploration in the same vein, see David Gill, *Becoming Good: Building Moral Character* (Downers Grove: InterVarsity Press, 2000).

[7] Luke renders this as "blessed are you who are poor" (Luke 6:20). Scholars have debated which of the two accounts is primary. Jesus opens his ministry in Luke 4:16–18 by reading from Isaiah 61:1, saying that he has come "to bring good news to the poor." When John the Baptist questions whether Jesus is the Messiah, Jesus replies, "the poor have good news brought to them" (Matt. 11:5). But other scholars point out that "the poor" are the humble and devout who seek God, which suggests that "poor in spirit" is the primary sense. This accords with Isaiah 66:2, "But this is the one to whom I will look, to the humble and contrite in spirit, who trembles at my word." Jesus references "the poor" fifteen times in the Gospels. Three times he refers to those who have nothing to eat, but eleven times he refers to the humble and pious who seek God. Perhaps the best resolution is that the biblical concept of the "poor" refers both to socioeconomic poverty and spiritual bankruptcy, and the consequent need to depend on God.

are those who realize they are spiritually bankrupt, for this realization turns them to God, without whom they cannot fulfill what they are created to do and be. Much of the rest of the sermon rips away from us the self-delusion that we are capable of acquiring a state of blessedness on our own. It aims to produce in us a genuine poverty of spirit.

What is the practical result of this blessing? If we are poor in spirit, we are able to bring an honest appraisal of ourselves to our work. We don't inflate our résumé or boast about our position. We know how difficult it is to work with people who cannot learn, grow, or accept correction because they are trying to maintain an inflated picture of themselves. So we commit ourselves to honesty about ourselves. We remember that even Jesus, when he started working with wood, must have needed guidance and instruction. At the same time, we acknowledge that only with God at work within us can we put Jesus' teachings into practice on the job. We seek God's presence and strength in our lives each day as we live as Christians where we work.

In the fallen world, poverty of spirit may seem to be a hindrance to success and advancement. Often this is an illusion. Who is likely to be more successful in the long run? A leader who says, "Fear not, I can handle anything, just do as I say," or a leader who says, "Together, we can do it, but everyone will have to perform better than ever before"? If there was ever a time when an arrogant, self-promoting leader was considered greater than a humble, empowering leader, that time is passing, at least within the best organizations. For example, a humble leader is the first characteristic mark of companies that achieve sustained greatness, according to Jim Collins's well-known research.[8] Of course, many workplaces remain stuck in the old kingdom of self-promotion and inflated self-appraisal. In some situations, the best practical advice may be to find another workplace if at all possible. In other cases, leaving the job may not be possible, or it may not be desirable, because by staying a Christian could be an important force for good. In these situations, the poor in spirit are all the more a blessing to those around them.

---

[8] Jim Collins, *Good to Great: Why Some Companies Make the Leap . . . And Others Don't* (New York: HarperBusiness, 2001), 20.

"Blessed Are Those Who Mourn, for They Will Be Comforted" (Matthew 5:4)

The second beatitude builds on our mental recognition of our poverty of spirit by adding an emotional response of sorrow. When we face the evil in our own lives, it saddens us; when we face the evil in the world—which includes possible evil in our workplace—that, too, touches our emotions with grief. The evil may come from ourselves, from others, or from sources unknown. In any case, when we honestly mourn evil words, evil deeds, or evil policies on the job, God sees our sorrow and comforts us with the knowledge that it will not always be this way.

Those blessed with mourning about their own failings can receive comfort at work by admitting their errors. If we make a mistake with a colleague, student, customer, employee, or other person, we admit it and ask their pardon. This takes courage! Without the emotional blessing of sadness over our actions, we would probably never muster the guts to admit our mistakes. But if we do, we may be surprised how often people are ready to forgive us. And if, on occasion, others take advantage of our admission of fault, we can fall back on the blessing of nonarrogance that flows from the first beatitudes.

Some businesses have found expressing sorrow to be an effective way to operate. Toro, the manufacturer of tractors and lawn equipment, adopted a practice of showing concern to people injured while using their products. As soon as the company learns of an injury, it contacts the injured person to express sorrow and offer help. It also asks for suggestions to improve the product. Surprising as it may sound, this approach has reduced the number of customer lawsuits over a period of many years.[9] Virginia Mason Hospital found similar results from acknowledging their role in patient deaths.[10]

"Blessed Are the Meek, for They Will Inherit the Earth" (Matthew 5:5)

The third beatitude puzzles many people in the workplace, in part because they don't understand what it means to be meek. Many assume the

[9] "Kendrick B. Melrose: Caring about People: Employees and Customers," *Ethix* 55 (Sept. 2007), http://ethix.org/2007/10/01/caring-about-people-employees-and-customers.

[10] "Dr. Gary Kaplan: Determined Steps to Transformation," *Ethix* 73 (Jan. 2001), http://ethix.org/2011/01/11/dr-gary-s-kaplan-determined-steps-to-transformation.

term means *weak, tame,* or *deficient in courage.* But the biblical understanding of meekness is power under control. In the Old Testament, Moses
was described as the meekest man on earth (Num. 12:3, KJV). Jesus described himself as "meek and lowly" (Matt. 11:28–29, KJV), which was consistent with his vigorous action in cleansing the temple (Matt. 21:12–13).

Power under God's control means two things: (1) refusal to inflate our
own self-estimation; and (2) reticence to assert ourselves *for* ourselves. Paul
captures the first aspect perfectly in Romans 12:3: "For by the grace given
to me I say to everyone among you not to think of yourself more highly than
you ought to think, but to think with sober judgment, each according to the
measure of faith that God has assigned." Meek people see themselves as
servants of God, not thinking more highly of themselves than they ought
to think. To be meek is to accept our strengths and limitations for what
they truly are, instead of constantly trying to portray ourselves in the best
possible light. But it does not mean that we should deny our strengths and
abilities. When asked if he was the Messiah, Jesus replied, "The blind receive their sight, the lame walk, the lepers are cleansed, the deaf hear, the
dead are raised, and the poor have good news brought to them. And blessed
is anyone who takes no offense at me" (Matt. 11:4–6). He had neither an
inflated self-image nor an inferiority complex, but a servant's heart based
on what Paul would later call "sober judgment" (Rom. 12:3).

A servant's heart is the crux of the second aspect of meekness: reticence to assert ourselves *for* ourselves. We exercise power, but for the
benefit of all people, not just ourselves. The second aspect is captured by
Psalm 37:1–11a, which begins with, "Do not fret because of the wicked,"
and ends with "the meek shall inherit the land." It means we curb our
urge to avenge the wrongs done against us, and instead use whatever
power we have to serve others. It flows from the sorrow for our own
weaknesses that comprises the second beatitude. If we feel sorrow for
our own sins, can we really feel vengeful over the sins of others?

It can be very challenging to put our power at work under God's
control. In the fallen world, it seems to be the aggressive and the self-
promoting who get ahead. "You don't get what you deserve, you get what
you negotiate."[11] In the workplace, the arrogant and powerful seem to

---

[11] Chester L. Karass, *In Business and in Life: You Don't Get What You Deserve, You Get What You Negotiate* (n.p.: Stanford Street Press, 1996).

win, but in the end they lose. They don't win in personal relationships. No one wants an arrogant, self-seeking friend. Men and women who are hungry for power are often lonely people. Nor do they win in financial security. They think they possess the world, but the world possesses them. The more money they have, the less financially secure they feel.

In contrast, Jesus said that the meek "will inherit the earth." As we have seen, the earth has become the location of the kingdom of heaven. We tend to think of the kingdom of heaven as *heaven*, a place completely different (golden streets, gates of pearl, a mansion over the hilltop) from anything we know here. But God's promise of the kingdom is a new heaven and a new *earth* (Rev. 21:1).

Those who submit their power to God will inherit the perfect kingdom coming to earth. In this kingdom, we receive by God's grace the good things the arrogant fruitlessly strive for in the present earth, and more. And this is not a future reality only. Even in a broken world, those who recognize their true strengths and weaknesses can find peace by living realistically. Those who exercise power for the benefit of *others* are often admired. The meek engage others in decision making and experience better results and deeper relationships.

"Blessed Are Those Who Hunger and Thirst for Righteousness, for They Will Be Filled" (Matthew 5:6)

Understanding the fourth beatitude turns on understanding what Jesus meant by *righteousness*. In ancient Judaism, to act righteously meant "to acquit, vindicate, restore to a right relationship."[12] The righteous are those who maintain right relationships—with God and with the people around them. On the basis of right relationships, those who commit infractions are acquitted of guilt.

Have you received the blessing of being filled with right relationships? It flows from meekness (the third beatitude) because we can only form right relationships with others when we cease making all our actions revolve around ourselves. Do you hunger and thirst for right relationships—with God, with your co-workers, with your family, and your

---

[12] David Noel Freedman, *The Anchor Yale Bible Dictionary* (New York: Doubleday, 1996), 5:737.

community? Hunger is a sign of life. We are genuinely hungry for good relationships if we yearn for others for their own sake, not just as snack food for meeting our own needs. If we see that we have God's grace for this, we will hunger and thirst for right relationships, not only with God, but with the people with whom we work or live.

Jesus says that those who have this hunger will find their appetites filled. It is easy to see the wrongs in our workplaces and to want to do battle to fix them. If we do this, we are hungering and thirsting for righteousness, desiring to see wrongs righted. The Christian faith has been the source of many of the greatest reforms in the work world, perhaps most notably the abolition of slavery in Great Britain and the United States, and the genesis of the Civil Rights movement. But again, the flow of the beatitudes is important. We don't take on these battles in our own strength, but only in recognition of our own emptiness, mourning our own unrighteousness, submitting our power to God.

"Blessed Are the Merciful, for They will Receive Mercy" (Matthew 5:7)

If you are blessed with sorrow for your own failings (the second beatitude) and with right relationships (the fourth beatitude), you will not find it difficult to show mercy to others on the job or anywhere else. Mercy consists of treating people better than they deserve from us. Forgiveness is a type of mercy. So is aiding someone whom we have no obligation to help, or forbearing to exploit someone's vulnerability. Mercy, in all these senses, is the driving force of Christ's incarnation, death, and resurrection. Through him, our sins are forgiven and we ourselves receive aid by the gift of God's spirit (1 Cor. 12). The Spirit's reason for showing us this mercy is simply that God loves us (John 3:16).

At work, mercy has a highly practical effect. We are to aid others to attain their best outcomes, regardless of how we feel about them. When you assist a co-worker, whom you may not like and who may have even wronged you in the past, you are showing mercy. When you are the first contestant in an audition and you warn the later contestants that the judge is in a foul mood, you are showing mercy, though it may give them an advantage over you. When a competitor's child is sick, and you agree to reschedule your presentation to the client so your competitor won't have to choose between caring for the child and competing for the business, you are showing mercy.

These kinds of mercy may cost you an advantage you could otherwise have taken. Yet they benefit the work outcome, as well as the other person. Assisting someone you don't like helps your work unit achieve its goals, even if it doesn't benefit *you* personally. Or—as in the case of the competitor with a sick child—if it doesn't benefit *your* organization, it benefits the client you aim to serve. The underlying reality of mercy is that mercy benefits someone beyond yourself.

An environment of forgiveness in an organization offers another surprising result. It improves the organization's performance. If someone makes a mistake in an organization where mercy is not shown, they are likely not to say anything about it, hoping it will not be noticed and they will not be blamed.

This diminishes performance in two ways. The first is that an error covered up may be much more difficult to deal with later. Imagine a construction job where a worker makes a mistake with a foundation fitting. It is easy to fix if it is brought to light and repaired right away. But it will be very expensive to fix after the structure is built and the foundation buried. The second is that the best learning experiences come out of learning from errors. As Soichiro Honda said, "Success can only be achieved through repeated failure and introspection. In fact, success represents the 1 percent of your work that only comes from the 99 percent that is called failure."[13] Organizations don't have the opportunity to learn if mistakes are not brought forward.

"Blessed Are the Pure in Heart, for They Will See God" (Matthew 5:8)

The sixth beatitude echoes Psalm 24:3–5:

> Who shall ascend the hill of the Lord?
>   And who shall stand in his holy place?
> Those who have clean hands and pure hearts,
>   who do not lift up their souls to what is false,
>   and do not swear deceitfully.
> They will receive blessing from the Lord,
>   and vindication from the God of their salvation.

---

[13] Tom Peters, *Thriving on Chaos* (New York: Knopf, 1987), 259–66.

"Clean hands and pure hearts" denote integrity, singleness of devotion, undivided loyalty. Integrity goes well beyond avoiding deceit and bad behavior. The root of integrity is wholeness, meaning that our actions are not choices we put on or take off as may seem convenient, but stem from the whole of our being. Notice that Jesus pronounces the blessing of being pure in heart not right after the blessing of hungering for righteousness, but after the blessing of showing mercy. Purity of heart arises not from perfection of our will, but from reception of God's grace.

We can determine how much of this blessing we have received by asking ourselves: How much commitment do I have to integrity, when I might be able to get away with skillful deception? Do I refuse to let my opinion of someone be shaped by gossip and innuendo, no matter how juicy? To what extent are my actions and words accurate reflections of what is in my heart?

It is hard to argue against personal integrity in the workplace, yet in a fallen world it is often the butt of jokes. Like mercy and meekness, it can be seen as weakness. But it is the person of integrity who will "see God." While the Bible is clear that God is invisible and "dwells in unapproachable light" (1 Tim. 1:17; 6:16), the pure in heart can perceive and sense God's reality in this life. In fact, without integrity, the deceits we propagate against others eventually make us unable to perceive the truth. We inevitably begin to believe our own fabrications. And this leads to ruin in the workplace, because work based on unreality soon becomes ineffective. The impure have no desire to see God, but those who are part of Christ's kingdom are blessed because they see reality as it truly is, including the reality of God.

"Blessed Are the Peacemakers, for They Will Be Called Children of God" (Matthew 5:9)

The seventh beatitude takes every Christian worker into the task of conflict resolution. Conflicts arise whenever people have differences of opinion. In a fallen world, the tendency is to ignore conflict or suppress it by using force, threat, or intimidation. But all of those are violations of the integrity (the sixth beatitude) of the people in conflict. In God's kingdom, it is a blessing to bring people together who are in conflict. Only then is it possible to resolve the conflict and restore the relationships.

(Later in this article, we will explore Jesus' method for conflict resolution in Matt. 18:17–19).

The result of conflict resolution is peace, and peacemakers will be called "children of God." They will reflect the divine character in their actions. God is the God of peace (1 Thess. 5:16) and we show ourselves to be his children when we seek to make peace in the workplace, in the community, in our homes, and in the whole world.

"Blessed Are Those Who Are Persecuted for Righteousness' Sake" (Matthew 5:10)

The eighth and final beatitude may strike us as negative. Up to this point, the beatitudes have focused on humility, meekness, right relationships, mercy, purity of heart, and peacemaking—all positive qualities. But Jesus includes the possibility of "persecution for righteousness' sake." This arises from the previous seven, because the forces that oppose God's ways still hold great power in the world.

Note that persecution arising from *unrighteous* behavior is not blessed. If we fail through our own fault, we should expect to suffer negative consequences. Jesus is talking about the blessing of being persecuted for doing right. But why would we be persecuted for righteousness? The reality in a fallen world is that if we demonstrate genuine righteousness, many will reject us. Jesus elaborates by pointing out that the prophets, who like him announced God's kingdom, were persecuted: "Blessed are you when people revile you and persecute you and utter all kinds of evil against you falsely on my account. Rejoice and be glad, for your reward is great in heaven, for in the same way they persecuted the prophets who were before you" (Matt. 5:11–12). Righteous people in the workplace may be subjected to active, even severe persecution by people who benefit—or believe they benefit—from injustice there.

For example, if you speak up for—or merely befriend—people who are victims of gossip or discrimination in your workplace, expect persecution. If you are the president of a trade association, and you speak out against an unfair subsidy your members are receiving, don't expect them to re-elect you. The blessing is that active persecution for the right reasons indicates that the powers of darkness believe you are succeeding in furthering God's kingdom.

Even the best organizations and most admirable people are still tainted by the Fall. None are perfect. The eighth beatitude serves as a reminder to us that working in a fallen world requires courage.

Salt and Light in the World of Work (Matthew 5:13–16)

Following the beatitudes in the Sermon on the Mount, Jesus tells his followers that people who receive these blessings *matter*:

> "You are the salt of the earth; but if salt has lost its taste, how can its saltiness be restored? It is no longer good for anything, but is thrown out and trampled under foot. You are the light of the world. A city built on a hill cannot be hid. No one after lighting a lamp puts it under the bushel basket, but on the lampstand, and it gives light to all in the house. In the same way, let your light shine before others, so that they may see your good works and give glory to your Father in heaven." (Matt. 5:13–16)

If you are a follower of Jesus living the beatitudes, you matter. You have an important role to play because you are the salt of the earth. Salt preserves and Christians help preserve what is good in the culture. In the ancient world, salt was very valuable: the Greeks thought it contained something almost divine, and the Romans sometimes paid their soldiers with salt. A soldier who didn't carry out his duties "was not worth his salt." You are a seasoning agent. In a sense, you can bring the distinctive flavor of God's values to all of life. You can make life palatable.

Note that salt, to be effective, must be in contact with the meat or fish it is to preserve. To be effective, we must be involved where we work and where we live. This puts us in a tension because the dominant culture doesn't necessarily like us. The majority of the time, living according to the beatitudes may make us more successful in work. But we need to be prepared for the times it doesn't. What will we do if showing mercy, making peace, or working for justice jeopardizes our position at work? Withdrawing from the world is no answer for Christians. But it is difficult to live in the world, ready to challenge its ways at any time. In Matthew 5:10–12, Jesus acknowledged the reality of persecution. But in our contacts with the culture, we must retain our "saltiness," our distinctiveness. It's a balancing act we're called upon to maintain.

"You are the light of the world." The job description of a Christian is not only to maintain personal holiness, but also to touch the lives of everyone around us. At work, we touch many people who do not encounter Christ in church. It may be our most effective place to witness to Christ. But we have to be careful about how we witness for Christ at work. We are being paid to do our work, and it would be dishonest to stint our employers by using work time for evangelism. Moreover, it would be dishonorable to create divisions at work or a hostile environment for nonbelievers. We must avoid any possible taint of seeking self-promotion by proselytizing. And we always run the risk that our failings at work may bring shame on the name of Christ, especially if we seem to be enthusiastic about evangelism but shoddy in actual work.

With all these dangers, how can we be salt and light at work? Jesus said our light is not necessarily in the witness of our words, but in the witness of our deeds—our "good works." "Let your light so shine before men that they may see your good deeds and glorify your Father who is in heaven." The beatitudes have spelled out some of those good works. In humility and submission to God, we work for right relations, for merciful actions, and for peace. When we live as people of blessing, we are salt and light—in the workplace, in our homes, and in our nation.

Living Out the "Righteousness" of the Kingdom of Heaven (Matthew 5:17–48)

Jesus makes a startling statement in Matthew 5:20: "I tell you, unless your righteousness exceeds that of the scribes and Pharisees, you will never enter the kingdom of heaven." Ordinary people in his day revered the apparent righteousness of the religious leaders and could not imagine ever matching them in their piety. Jesus shocks them by stating that entrance into God's kingdom was available only to those whose righteousness exceeded that of the scribes and Pharisees. Who, then, could be saved? The problem lay in equating righteousness with external piety, a common understanding of the word both then and now. But the word *righteousness* throughout the Bible (as noted above in the fourth beatitude) always denotes right relationships—with God and with people around us. This includes those in the workplace.

This becomes plain in the illustrations that follow. In Matthew 5:21–26, it is not enough not to murder someone; we must guard against harboring anger that leads to insults and broken relationships. We may feel anger, but the right way to handle anger is try to resolve conflict (Matt. 18:15–19), not to push the person away with insults or slander. Jesus is clear that a right relationship between you and your brother or sister is so vital that you should forego religious practices until you have cleared the matter between the two of you.

In the workplace, anger may be used to manipulate others. Or anger may overwhelm you because you feel unfairly treated. Deal with the issue: take the first step toward reconciliation, even though it may put you in a position of humility. Engaging in fair, open conflict resolution is the way of the new kingdom. Again, blessed are the peacemakers.

Wealth and Provision (Matthew 6)

Jesus speaks about wealth frequently. Wealth and provision are not in themselves work, but they are often the result of work, our own or someone else's. A central tenet of economics is that the purpose of work is to increase wealth, making this a work-related topic. Here are Jesus' teachings on wealth and daily provision as they appear in the Sermon on the Mount.

"Give Us This Day Our Daily Bread" (Matthew 6:11)

Immediately before this request for daily bread in the Lord's Prayer, we read, "Your kingdom come. Your will be done, on earth as it is in heaven" (Matt. 6:10). In God's kingdom, receiving our daily bread is a certainty, but in our world marred by sin, daily sustenance is questionable. Although God has given humanity everything we need to produce enough food to feed everyone on earth, we have not ended hunger. Thus Jesus' first word about wealth or daily provision is this petition: "Give us this day our daily bread." We turn to God for the bread we need.

But note that the petition is plural: Give *us* this day *our* daily bread. We don't pray only for our own bread, but for bread for those who have none. As people longing to maintain right relationships with others, we take others' need of bread into consideration: we share what we have with those who have need. If every person, business, institution, and government worked according to the purposes and principles of God's kingdom, no one would be hungry.

Store Your Treasure in Heaven, Not on Earth (Matthew 6:19–34)

Not only are we to ask God for our daily provision, but we also are warned against stockpiling material wealth and other treasures on earth:

> "Do not store up for yourselves treasures on earth, where moth and rust consume and where thieves break in and steal; but store up for yourselves treasures in heaven, where neither moth nor rust consumes and where thieves do not break in and steal. For where your treasure is, there your heart will be also." (Matt. 6:19–21)

"Treasures in heaven" is not a vaporous reference to kindly thoughts in God's heart or some such platitude. God's kingdom will ultimately rule on earth. "Treasures in heaven" are things of worth in God's coming kingdom, such as justice, opportunity for everyone to be productive, provision for everyone's needs, and respect for the dignity of every person. The implication is that we would do better to invest our money in activities that transform the world, than in securities that protect our accumulated surplus.

Is it wrong, then, to have a retirement portfolio or even to care about the material things of this world for ourselves or for others? The answer is again both no and yes. The *no* comes from the fact that this passage is not the only one in the Bible speaking to questions of wealth and provision for those who are dependent on us. Other passages counsel prudence and forethought, such as, "Those who gather little by little will increase [wealth]" (Prov. 13:11b), and, "The good leave an inheritance to their children's children" (Prov. 13:22). God guides Joseph to store up food for seven years in advance of a famine (Gen. 41:25–36), and Jesus speaks favorably in the parable of the talents (Matt. 25:14–30, which will be discussed later) of investing money. In light of the rest of Scripture, Matthew 6:19–34 cannot be a blanket prohibition.

But the *yes* part of the answer is a warning, summed up beautifully in verse 21: "Where your treasure is, there will your heart be also."

We might expect this sentence to run the other way: "Where your heart is, there your treasure will be also." But Jesus' actual words are more profound. Money changes the heart more than the heart decides how to handle money. Jesus' point is not "You tend to put your money into things that matter to you," but, "The possessions you own will change you so that you care more about them than about other things." Choose carefully what you own, for you will inevitably begin to value and protect it, to the potential detriment of everything else.

We may call this the "Treasure Principle," namely, that *treasure transforms*. Those who invest their deepest treasure in the things of this world will find they are no longer serving God but money (Matt. 6:24). That can lead to anxiety coming from the uncertainties of money (Matt. 6:25–34). Will it be eroded by inflation? Will the stock market crash? Will the bonds default? Will the bank fail? Can I be sure that what I've saved will be enough to handle anything that could possibly happen?

The antidote is to invest in ways that meet people's genuine needs. A company that provides clean water or well-made clothes may be investing in the kingdom of God, whereas an investment that depends on politically motivated subsidies, overheated housing markets, or material shortages may not. This passage in Matthew 6 is not a rule for portfolio management, but it does tell us that our commitment to the ways and means of God's kingdom extends to how we manage such wealth as we have.

The question, then, is what kind of attention you should pay to material needs and the accumulation of resources. If you pay *anxious* attention, you are foolish. If you let them *displace your trust in God*, you are becoming unfaithful. If you pay *excessive* attention to them, you will become greedy. If you acquire them *at the expense of other people,* you are becoming the kind of oppressor against whom God's kingdom is pitched.

How are we to discern the line between appropriate and inappropriate attention to wealth? Jesus answers, "Strive first for the kingdom of God and his righteousness, and all these things will be given to you" (Matt. 6:33). First things first. Despite our large capacity for self-deception, this question can help us observe carefully where our treasure has put us. That will tell us something about our hearts.

Moral Guidance (Matthew 7)

"Do Not Judge, So That You May Not Be Judged" (Matthew 7:1–5)

Jesus calls us to realism about ourselves that will keep us from picking at or judging someone else:

> "Do not judge, so that you may not be judged. For with the judgment you make you will be judged, and the measure you give will be the measure you get. Why do you see the speck in your neighbor's eye, but do not notice the log in your own eye? Or how can you say to your neighbor, 'Let me take the speck out of your eye,' while the log is in your own eye? You hypocrite, first take the log out of your own eye, and then you will see clearly to take the speck out of your neighbor's eye." (Matt. 7:1–5)

This may seem to pose a problem in the workplace. Successful work often depends on making assessments of other people's character and work. Bosses must assess their subordinates, and in some organizations, vice versa. We must often decide whom to trust, whom to choose as partners, whom to employ, which organization to join. But verse 5, with the word *hypocrite* and the admonition, "First take the log out of your own eye," shows that Jesus is speaking against false or unnecessary judgment, not against honest assessment. The problem is that we are constantly making judgments unaware. The mental pictures we make of others in our workplaces are composed more of our biased perceptions than of reality. Partly, this is because we see in others whatever serves to make us feel better about ourselves. Partly, it is to justify our own actions when we do not act as servants to others. Partly, it is because we lack the time or inclination to collect true information, which is much harder to do than storing up random impressions.

It may be impossible to overcome this false judgmentalism on our own. This is why consistent, fact-based assessment systems are so important in workplaces. A good performance appraisal system requires managers to gather real evidence of performance, to discuss differing perceptions with employees, and to recognize common biases. On a personal level, between those who are not one another's bosses, we can ac-

complish some of the same impartiality by asking ourselves "What role
do I have in that?" when we notice ourselves forming a judgment against
someone else. "What evidence leads me to that conclusion? How does
this judgment benefit me? What would that person say in response to
this judgment?" Perhaps the surest way to remove the log in our own
eye is to take our judgment directly to the other person and ask them
to respond to our perception. (See the section on conflict resolution in
Matthew 18:15–17.)

The Golden Rule (Matthew 7:12)

"In everything do to others as you would have them do to you; for
this is the law and the prophets" (Matt. 7:12). This brings us back to true
righteousness, the mending and sustaining of right relationships on the
job as well as elsewhere. If we have time for only one question before
making a decision-taking action, the best one may be, "Is this how I
would want it to be done to me?"

Lord, Have Mercy (Matthew 8–9)

In chapters 5 through 7, we heard Jesus teaching about the kingdom
of heaven coming to earth. In chapters 8 through 9, we see him enact-
ing that kingdom through deeds of compassion and mercy. He heals
an ostracized leper (Matt. 8:1–4), he has compassion on an officer of
the Roman occupying forces (Matt. 8:5–20), and he delivers demoni-
acs sitting in the midst of a perfect storm of misery (Matt. 8:28–9:1).
In all these cases, Jesus' compassion leads him to act to reclaim God's
creation. The compassion of his followers can be expressed in equally
practical ways.

As Jesus demonstrates the coming of the kingdom, he calls those
who follow him "laborers" (Matt. 9:37–38). Some of us are led to work in
physical and emotional healing, similar to Jesus' work in these chapters.
Others are led to work in occupations that provide food, water, shelter,
transportation, education, health care, justice, safety, or good government, similar to Jesus' work providing wooden goods until he was about

thirty. Given the time Jesus spent healing people, it is surprising that most people think of him as a preacher rather than as a doctor. Still others are led to express their creativity in art, entrepreneurism, design, fashion, research and development, made as we are in the image of a creative God (Gen. 1). The point is that for Jesus there is no separation between the secular and the sacred, between the spiritual and physical aspects of announcing the kingdom of God.

Laborers Deserve Their Food (Matthew 10)

In chapter 10, Jesus sends out his disciples to proclaim the coming kingdom and to demonstrate it through powerful deeds of mercy and compassion. He instructs them to make no provision for their needs (Matt. 10:9–10), but instead to depend on the generosity of others. He is clear that the gospel is not to become a matter of commerce: "You received without payment; give without payment" (Matt. 10:8).

The lesson here for us is that earning money and thinking about finances are not bad; indeed, it is through our labor that God provides for us, for "the laborers deserve their food" (Matt. 10:10). But the warning is against allowing our earnings to become our primary focus at work. As workers under the Lord of the new kingdom, our primary focus is on the value of the work, not on the paycheck. Jesus' instructions here are meant to keep God in the forefront of our hearts (cf. James 4:13–16). Whatever the signature at the bottom of our paycheck, God is ultimately underwriting it all.

Tales of Two Kingdoms (Matthew 11–17)

As we walk through Matthew's Gospel, we see that opposition to Jesus—his message and his actions—is increasing. It culminates in Matthew 12:14 with the religious leaders' decision to stop him, even if it means killing him. This foreshadows and sets in motion the end to which the whole narrative is pointing: Jesus' crucifixion in Jerusalem. Knowing what lies ahead of him, Jesus nevertheless tells his followers,

"Come to me, all you that are weary and are carrying heavy burdens, and I will give you rest. Take my yoke upon you, and learn from me; for I am gentle and humble in heart, and you will find rest for your souls. For my yoke is easy, and my burden is light." (Matt. 11:28–30)

If we do our work in yoke with him, we will find fulfillment and experience good relationships with God and people.[14] When God gave work to Adam in the Garden of Eden, the work was easy and the burden light under God's authority. When the human pair rebelled against their Maker, the character of work changed to hard labor against thorns and thistles (Gen. 3). Jesus invites us to work in yoke with him with the promise of rest for our souls. (For more on working in yoke with Christ, see "2 Corinthians 6:14–18" in "2 Corinthians and Work.")

Working on the Sabbath (Matthew 12:1–8)

One of the chief areas of conflict between Jesus and his opponents was in keeping the Sabbath. In this passage, Jesus is criticized by religious leaders for allowing his followers to pluck and eat grain on the Sabbath. The Pharisees regarded this as work, which was forbidden on the Sabbath. Jesus dismisses both their interpretation and their motivation. He argues that plucking just enough grain to satisfy immediate hunger does not break the Sabbath, because both King David and the temple priests did so without incurring God's rebuke (Matt. 12:3–5). Moreover, true adherence to the Law of Moses should be motivated by compassion and mercy (Matt. 12:6). God's love of mercy (allowing hungry people to pick grain to eat) is higher than God's desire for sacrifice (following Sabbath regulations), as had already been revealed in Micah 6:6–8. The gift of a day of rest each week is a promise from God that we do not have to work incessantly just to make ends meet. It is not a judgment against relieving someone's hunger or need on the Sabbath.

The connection between the Jewish Sabbath and the Christian worship on Sunday, and the application of Jewish Sabbath law to the Christian life are discussed in greater depth in the sections on "Mark 1:21–45"

[14] Frederick Dale Bruner, *The Christbook, Matthew 1–12*, vol. 1, *Matthew: A Commentary* (Grand Rapids: Wm. B. Eerdmans, 2007), 537–40.

and "Mark 2:23–3:6" in "Mark and Work," and the sections on "Luke 6:1–11; 3:10–17" in "Luke and Work."

Parables of the Kingdom (Matthew 13)

Beginning in chapter 13, in the face of opposition, Jesus' teaching style changes. Instead of proclaiming the kingdom clearly, he begins to speak in parables that are meaningful to believers but incomprehensible to unbelievers. Most of these brief stories are about workers: a sower planting a field (Matt. 13:3–9); a woman kneading yeast into bread (Matt. 13:33); a treasure hunter (Matt. 13:44); a pearl merchant (Matt. 13:45–46); some fishermen (Matt. 13:47–50); and a householder (Matt. 13:52). For the most part, these stories are not about the work they depict. Jesus does not tell us how to properly sow a field, how to bake bread, or how to invest in commodities. Instead, Jesus uses material objects and human labor as elements of stories that give us insight into God's kingdom. Our work is capable of bearing meaning, even of illustrating eternal realities. This reminds us that we and the world around us spring from God's creation and remain parts of God's kingdom.

Paying Taxes (Matthew 17:24–27 and 22:15–22)

In Jesus' day, Jews paid taxes both locally to the Jewish temple and to the pagan government in Rome. Matthew records two separate instances depicting Jesus' view on paying these taxes. The first incident is recorded in Matthew 17:24–27, where the collectors of the temple tax ask Peter whether Jesus pays that tax. Jesus, knowing of this conversation, asks Peter, "What do you think, Simon? From whom do kings of the earth take toll or tribute? From their children or from others?" Peter answers, "From others." Jesus responds, "Then the children are free. However, so that we do not give offense to them, go to the sea and cast a hook; take the first fish that comes up; and when you open its mouth, you will find a coin; take that and give it to them for you and me."

The second incident, concerning the Roman tax, is found in Matthew 22:15–22. Here the Pharisees and Herodians want to entrap Jesus with the question, "Is it lawful to pay taxes to the emperor, or not?" Jesus knows the malice in their hearts and responds with a cutting question:

"Why are you putting me to the test, you hypocrites? Show me the coin used for the tax." When they hand him a denarius, he asks, "Whose head is this, and whose title?" They respond, "The emperor's." Jesus ends the conversation with the words, "Give therefore to the emperor the things that are the emperor's, and to God the things that are God's."

Our true citizenship is in God's kingdom, and we devote our resources to God's purposes. But we give to earthly powers what is due. Paying taxes is one of the bedrock obligations we as citizens or residents undertake for the services we enjoy in any civilized society. Those services include the work of first responders (police, firefighters, medical people, and so on), as well as the social nets in place to assure justice or aid for the poor, the aged, and others in need. The Roman Empire was not governed primarily for the benefit of the common people, yet even so it provided roads, water, policing, and sometimes relief for the poor. We may not always agree on the type or extent of services our governments should provide, but we know that our taxes are essential in providing for our personal protection and for the help of those who cannot help themselves.

Even though not all of government activity serves God's purposes, Jesus does not call us to flout the tax requirements of the nations where we reside (Rom. 13:1–10; 1 Thess. 4:11–12). Jesus is saying in essence that we do not necessarily have to resist paying taxes as a matter of principle. When possible, we should "live peaceably with all" (Rom. 12:18; Heb. 12:14; cf. 1 Pet. 2:12), while also living as lights shining in the darkness (Matt. 5:13–16; Phil. 2:15). To work at our jobs and to refuse to pay our taxes in a way that brings dishonor to God's kingdom would be neither peaceable nor winsome.

This has direct applications to work. Workplaces are subject to governmental laws and powers, in addition to taxes. Some governments have laws and practices that may violate Christian purposes and ethics, as was true of Rome in the first century. Governments or their employees may demand bribes, impose unethical rules and regulations, subject people to suffering and injustice, and use the taxes for purposes contrary to God's will. As with taxes, Jesus does not demand that we resist every one of these abuses. We are like spies or guerrillas in enemy territory. We can't get bogged down in fighting the enemy kingdom at every stronghold. Instead, we must act strategically, always asking what will most further the establishment of God's kingdom on earth. Of course, we must never *engage* in abusive practices for our own benefit. (This topic is also discussed under "Luke 19:1–10; 20:20–26" in "Luke and Work.")

Living in the New Kingdom (Matthew 18–25)

In chapters 18 through 25 of Matthew's Gospel, Jesus gives concrete images of what life in God's kingdom is like. In many cases, these pictures apply particularly to work.

Conflict Resolution (Matthew 18:15–35)

All workplaces experience conflict. In this passage, Jesus gives us a template for dealing with someone who has wronged us. He does not say, "Get even!" or "Strike back!" Instead, he lays out a process that begins with seeking one-on-one to be reconciled. The beatitude of meekness means putting aside your self-justification long enough to express yourself respectfully and factually to the one who has hurt you, and to open yourself to their perspective (Matt. 18:15). This does not mean submitting to further abuse, but opening yourself to the possibility that your perception is not universal. But suppose that doesn't resolve the conflict? The fallback second step is to ask people who know you both to go with you as you take up the issue again with the person who caused pain or injury. If the conflict still is not resolved, then bring the matter to the leadership (the church, in Matthew 18:16, which is addressing church conflict specifically) for an impartial judgment. If that judgment doesn't resolve the issue, the offender who fails to abide by the judgment is removed from the community (Matt. 18:17).

Although Jesus was speaking about conflict with "another member of the church" (Matt. 18:15), his method is a remarkable precursor to what is now recognized as best practice in the workplace. Even in the finest workplaces, conflicts arise. When they do, the only effective resolution is for those in conflict to engage each other directly, not to complain to others. Rather than play out a personal conflict in front of an audience, get with the person privately. In the age of electronic communication, Jesus' approach is more important than ever. All it takes is a name or two in the "cc:" line or one press of the "reply all" button to turn a simple disagreement into an office feud. Even though two people could keep an e-mail chain to themselves, the possibilities for misunderstanding are multiplied when an impersonal medium such as e-mail is used. It might be best to take Jesus' advice literally: "Go and point out the fault when the two of you are alone" (Matt. 18:15).

Pointing out the fault is a two-way street. We need to be open to hearing faults pointed out to us as well. Listening—Jesus mentions listening *three times* in these three verses—is the crucial element. Contemporary conflict resolution models usually focus on getting the parties to listen to each other, even while preserving the option to disagree. Often, attentive listening leads to the discovery of a mutually acceptable resolution. If it doesn't, then others with the appropriate skills and authority are asked to get involved.

The Rich Young Man (Matthew 19:16–30)

The issue of money, discussed earlier in Matthew 6, raises its head again with the story of the rich young man who was drawn to Jesus. The young man asks Jesus, "What good deed must I do to have eternal life?" Jesus tells him to keep the commandments, and he responds that he has done that from his youth. A distinctive element in Matthew's narrative is that the young man then asks Jesus, "What do I still lack?" He shows great insight in asking this question. We can do everything that appears right but still know that something is not right on the inside. Jesus responds, "Sell your possessions and give the money to the poor, and you will have treasure in heaven; then come, follow me" (Matt. 19:21).

We know from the four Gospels that Jesus did not call all of his hearers to give away all their possessions. Not all people are as burdened by their possessions as this young man was. In his case, the challenge was radical because of his strong attachment to wealth (Matt. 19:22). God knows precisely what is in our hearts and what is needed as we serve him.

Is our treasure in our work, our jobs, our performance and skills, our retirement funds? These are good things (gifts from God) in their place. But they are secondary to seeking first the kingdom of God (Matt. 6:33) and a right (righteous) relationship with God and with others. We hold our wealth and our work on an open palm lest, like the rich young man, we end up turning away sorrowfully from God. (This story is discussed in greater depth in the entries for "Mark 10:17–31" and "Luke 18:18–30.")

The Laborers in the Vineyard (Matthew 20:1–16)

This parable is unique to Matthew's Gospel. The owner of a vineyard hires day laborers at various times throughout the day. The ones hired at six o'clock in the morning put in a full day's work. Those hired at five o'clock in the afternoon put in only one hour of work. But the owner pays everyone a full day's wage (a denarius). He goes out of his way to make sure that everyone knows that all are paid the same in spite of the different number of hours worked. Not surprisingly, those hired first complain that they worked longer but earned no more money than those who started late in the day.

> "But [the owner] replied to one of them, 'Friend, I am doing you no wrong; did you not agree with me for the usual daily wage? . . . Am I not allowed to do what I choose with what belongs to me? Or are you envious because I am generous?' So the last will be first, and the first will be last." (Matt. 20:13, 15–16)

Unlike the parable of the sower (Matt. 13:3–9; 18–23), Jesus does not give us an explicit interpretation. As a result, scholars have offered many interpretations. Because the people in the story are laborers and managers, some assume it is about work. In that case, it seems to say, "Don't compare your pay to others" or "Don't be dissatisfied if others get paid more or work less than you do in a similar job." It could be argued that these are good practices for workers. If you earn a decent wage, why make yourself miserable because others have it even better? But this interpretation of the parable can also be used to justify unfair or abusive labor practices. Some workers may receive lower wages for unfair reasons, such as race or sex or immigrant status. Does Jesus mean that we should be content when we or other workers are treated unfairly?

Moreover, paying people the same regardless of how much work they do is a questionable business practice. Wouldn't it give a strong incentive to all workers to show up at five o'clock in the afternoon the next day? And what about making everyone's pay public? It does reduce the scope for intrigue. But is it a good idea to force those working longer hours to watch while those who worked only one hour are paid an identical wage? It seems calculated to cause labor strife. Pay for nonperformance, to take the parable literally, doesn't seem to be a recipe for business success. Can it really be that Jesus advocates this pay practice?

Perhaps the parable is not really about work. The context is that Jesus is giving surprising examples of those who belong to God's kingdom: for example, children (Matt. 19:14) who legally don't even own themselves. He is clear that the kingdom does not belong to the rich, or at least not to very many of them (Matt. 19:23–26). It belongs to those who follow him, in particular if they suffer loss. "Many who are first will be last, and the last will be first" (Matt. 19:30). The present parable is followed immediately by another ending with the same words: "the first will be last, and the last will be first" (Matt. 20:16). This suggests that the story is a continuation of the discussion about those to whom the kingdom belongs. Entry into God's kingdom is not gained by our work or action, but by the generosity of God.

Once we understand the parable to be about God's generosity in the kingdom of heaven, we may still ask how it applies to work. If you are being paid fairly, the advice about being content with your wage may stand. If another worker receives an unexpected benefit, wouldn't it be graceful to rejoice, rather than grumble?

But there is also a broader application. The owner in the parable pays all the workers enough to support their families.[15] The social situation in Jesus' day was that many small farmers were being forced off their land because of debt they incurred to pay Roman taxes. This violated the God of Israel's command that land could not be taken away from the people who work it (Lev. 25:8–13), but of course this was of no concern to the Romans. Consequently, large pools of unemployed men gathered each morning, hoping to be hired for the day. They are the displaced,

---

[15] A denarius was the standard one-day wage in first-century Palestine.

unemployed, and underemployed workers of their day. Those still waiting at five o'clock have little chance of earning enough to buy food for their families that day. Yet the vineyard owner pays even them a full day's wage.

If the vineyard owner represents God, this is a powerful message that in God's kingdom, displaced and unemployed workers find work that meets their needs and the needs of those who depend on them. We have already seen Jesus saying that "laborers deserve their food" (Matt. 10:10). This does not necessarily mean that earthly employers have a responsibility for meeting all the needs of their employees. Earthly employers are not God. Rather, the parable is a message of hope to everyone struggling to find adequate employment. In God's kingdom, we will all find work that meets our needs. The parable is also a challenge to those who have a hand in shaping the structures of work in today's society. Can Christians do anything to advance this aspect of God's kingdom right now?

Servant Leadership (Matthew 20:20–28)

Despite this parable of God's grace and generosity, despite hearing Jesus remark twice that the first shall be last and the last first, Jesus' disciples are still missing the point. The mother of James and John asks Jesus to grant her two sons the most prominent places in his coming kingdom. The two men are standing there and Jesus turns to them and asks, "Are you able to drink the cup that I am about to drink?" They respond, "We are able." When the other ten disciples hear about this, they are angry. Jesus takes this opportunity to challenge their notions about prominence.

> "You know that the rulers of the Gentiles lord it over them, and their great ones are tyrants over them. It will not be so among you; but whoever wishes to be great among you must be your servant, and whoever wishes to be first among you must be your slave; just as the Son of Man came not to be served but to serve, and to give his life a ransom for many." (Matt. 20:25–28)

True leadership is found in serving others. What this looks like will vary according to the workplace and situation. This doesn't mean that a CEO must take a monthly turn sweeping the floors or cleaning the toilets, nor that any worker can cite helping someone else as an excuse for not doing their own work well. It does mean that we do all our work with the aim of serving our customers, co-workers, shareholders, and others whom our work affects. Max De Pree was a long time CEO of Herman Miller and member of the *Fortune* Hall of Fame. He wrote in his book *Leadership Is an Art*, "The first responsibility of a leader is to define reality. The last is to say thank you. In between the two, the leader must become a servant and a debtor. That sums up the progress of an artful leader."[16]

The servant is the person who knows his or her spiritual poverty (Matt. 5:3) and exercises power under God's control (Matt. 5:5) to maintain right relationships. The servant leader apologizes for mistakes (Matt. 5:4), shows mercy when others fail (Matt. 5:7), makes peace when possible (Matt. 5:9), and endures unmerited criticism when attempting to serve God (Matt. 5:10) with integrity (Matt. 5:8). Jesus set the pattern in his own actions on our behalf (Matt. 20:28). We show ourselves to be Christ-followers by following his example.

Words and Deeds (Matthew 21:28–41)

The parable of the two sons (Matt. 21:28–32) is about two brothers whose father tells them to go work in his vineyard. One tells his father that he will but doesn't do it. The other tells his father that he won't go but ends up working all day among the vines. Jesus then asks the question: "Which of the two did the will of his father?" The answer is clear: the one who actually worked, though initially refusing to do so. This parable continues earlier stories in Matthew about the people who actually are part of God's kingdom. Jesus tells the religious leaders in his audience that "tax collectors and prostitutes are going into the kingdom of God ahead of you" (Matt. 21:31).[17] The folks who look the least religious will enter God's kingdom ahead of religious leaders, because in the end they do God's will.

---

[16] Max De Pree, *Leadership Is an Art* (New York: Doubleday, 1989), 9.

[17] Jesus illustrates this in 21:32: The religious leaders had listened to John the Baptist but scorned him; tax collectors listened to him, believed, repented, and were baptized. But the religious leaders refused to hear the prophet's message or to repent, excluding themselves from God's kingdom.

In work, this reminds us that actions speak louder than words. Many organizations have mission statements declaring that their top aims are customer service, product quality, civic integrity, putting their people first, and the like. Yet many such organizations have poor service, quality, integrity, and employee relations. Individuals may do the same thing, extolling their plans, yet failing to implement them. Organizations and individuals falling into this trap may have good intentions, and they may not recognize they are failing to live up to their rhetoric. Workplaces need both effective systems for implementing their mission and goals, and impartial monitoring systems to give unvarnished feedback.

The parable immediately following the parable of the wicked tenants (Matt. 21:33–41) takes place in a workplace, namely, a vineyard. However, Jesus makes it clear that he is not talking about running a vineyard, but about his own rejection and coming murder at the instigation of the Jewish religious authorities of his day (Matt. 21:45). The key to applying it to today's workplace is verse 43: "The kingdom of God will be taken away from you and given to a people that produces the fruits of the kingdom." We all have been given responsibilities in our work. If we refuse to do them in obedience to God, we are working at odds with God's kingdom. In every job, our ultimate performance appraisal comes from God.

Serving Upward and Downward (Matthew 24:45–51)

This parable is about a slave who has been put in charge of the entire household. This includes the responsibility to give other slaves their allowance of food at the proper time. Jesus says, "Blessed is that slave whom his master will find at work when he arrives" (Matt. 24:46). That slave will be promoted to additional responsibility. On the other hand, Jesus observes,

> "But if that wicked slave says to himself, 'My master is delayed,' and he begins to beat his fellow slaves, and eats and drinks with drunkards, the master of that slave will come on a day when he does not expect him and at an hour that he does not know. He will cut him in pieces and put him with the hypocrites, where there will be weeping and gnashing of teeth." (Matt. 24:48–51)

In a modern workplace context, the slave would be equivalent to a manager with a duty to the owners while managing other workers. The owner's interests are met only when the workers' needs are met. The manager has responsibilities to both those above and below him in authority. Jesus says that it is the servant-leader's duty to look to the needs of those under him as well as those above him. He cannot excuse himself for mistreating those under his authority by claiming it is somehow for the benefit of his superiors. He depicts this reality dramatically in the punishment meted out to the worker who cares only for his own interests (Matt. 24:48–51).

The Parable of the Talents (Matthew 25:14–30)

One of Jesus' most significant parables regarding work is set in the context of investments (Matt. 25:14–30). A rich man delegates the management of his wealth to his servants, much as investors in today's markets do. He gives five talents (a large unit of money)[18] to the first servant, two talents to the second, and one talent to the third. Two of the servants earn 100 percent returns by trading with the funds, but the third servant hides the money in the ground and earns nothing. The rich man returns, rewards the two who made money, but severely punishes the servant who did nothing.

The meaning of the parable extends far beyond financial investments. God has given each person a wide variety of gifts, and he expects us to employ those gifts in his service. It is not acceptable merely to put those gifts on a closet shelf and ignore them. Like the three servants, we do not have gifts of the same degree. The return God expects of us is commensurate with the gifts we have been given. The servant who received

---

[18] According to NRSV footnote *f*, "a talent was worth more than 15 years' wages of a laborer," in other words, about $US 1 million in today's currency. The Greek word *talanton* was first used for a unit of weight (probably about 30–40 kg.), then later for a unit of money equivalent to the same weight of gold, silver (probably what is meant here), or copper (Donald A. Hagner, *Matthew 14–18*, vol. 33b, *Word Biblical Commentary* [Nashville: Thomas Nelson, 1995]). The present-day use of the English word *talent* to indicate an ability or gift is derived from this parable (Walter C. Kaiser Jr. and Duane Garrett, eds., *Archaeological Study Bible* [Grand Rapids: Zondervan, 2006], 1608.)

one talent was not condemned for failing to reach the five-talent goal; he was condemned because he did nothing with what he was given. The gifts we receive from God include skills, abilities, family connections, social positions, education, experiences, and more. The point of the parable is that we are to use whatever we have been given for God's purposes. The severe consequences to the unproductive servant, far beyond anything triggered by mere business mediocrity, tell us that we are to invest our lives, not waste them.

Yet the particular talent invested in the parable is *money*, on the order of a million U.S. dollars in today's world. In modern English, this fact is obscured because the word *talent* has come to refer mainly to skills or abilities. But this parable concerns money. It depicts investing, not hoarding, as a godly thing to do if it accomplishes godly purposes in a godly manner. In the end, the master praises the two trustworthy servants with the words, "Well done, good and trustworthy slave" (Matt. 25:23). In these words, we see that the master cares about the results ("well done"), the methods ("good"), and the motivation ("trustworthy").

More pointedly for the workplace, it commends putting capital at risk in pursuit of earning a return. Sometimes Christians speak as if growth, productivity, and return on investment were unholy to God. But this parable overturns that notion. We should invest our skills and abilities, but also our wealth and the resources made available to us at work, all for the affairs of God's kingdom. This includes the production of needed goods and services. The volunteer who teaches Sunday school is fulfilling this parable. So are the entrepreneur who starts a new business and gives jobs to others, the health service administrator who initiates an AIDS-awareness campaign, and the machine operator who develops a process innovation.

God does not endow people with identical or necessarily equal gifts. If you do as well as you can with the gifts given to you by God, you will hear his "Well done." Not only the gifts, but also the people have equal worth. At the same time, the parable ends with the talent taken from the third servant being given to the one with ten talents. Equal worth does not necessarily mean equal compensation. Some positions require more skill or ability and thus are compensated accordingly. The two servants who did well are rewarded in different amounts. But they are both praised identically. The implication of the parable is that we are to use whatever talents we've been given to the best of our ability for God's glory, and when we have done that, we are on an equal playing field with other faithful, trustworthy servants of God. (For a discussion of the highly similar parable of the ten minas see "Luke 19:11–27" in "Luke and Work.")

Sheep and Goats (Matthew 25:31–46)

Jesus' final teaching in this section examines how we treat those in need. In this account, when Jesus returns in his glory, he will sit on his throne and separate people "as a shepherd separates the sheep from the goats" (Matt. 25:32). The separation depends on how we treat people in need. To the sheep he says,

> "Come, you that are blessed by my Father, inherit the kingdom prepared for you from the foundation of the world; for I was hungry and you gave me food, I was thirsty and you gave me something to drink, I was a stranger and you welcomed me, I was naked and you gave me clothing, I was sick and you took care of me, I was in prison and you visited me." (Matt. 25:34–36)

These are all people in need, whom the sheep served, for Jesus says, "Just as you did it to one of the least of these who are members of my family, you did it to me" (Matt. 25:40). To the goats, he says,

> "Depart from me . . . for I was hungry and you gave me no food, I was thirsty and you gave me nothing to drink, I was a stranger and you did not welcome me, naked and you did not give me clothing, sick and in prison and you did not visit me. . . . Just as you did not do it to one of the least of these, you did not do it to me." (Matt. 25:41–43, 45)

Individually and corporately, we are called to help those in need. We are "bound in the bundle of the living under the care of the LORD your God" (1 Sam. 25:29), and we cannot ignore the plight of human beings suffering hunger, thirst, nakedness, homelessness, sickness, or imprisonment. We work in order to meet our own needs and the needs of those dependent on us; but we also work in order to have something to give to those in need (Heb. 13:1–3). We join with others to find ways to come alongside those who lack the basic necessities of life that we may take for granted. If Jesus' words in this passage are taken seriously, more may hang on our charity than we realize.

Jesus does not say exactly *how* the sheep served people in need. It may have been through gifts and charitable work. But perhaps some of it was through the ordinary work of growing and preparing food and drink; helping new co-workers come up to speed on the job; designing, manufacturing, and selling clothing. All legitimate work serves people who need the products and services of the work, and in so doing, serves Jesus.

The Body of Christ (Matthew 26)

The plot to kill Jesus moves forward as Judas (one of the Twelve) goes to the religious leaders with an offer to turn him over to the temple soldiers. With events moving quickly toward crucifixion, Jesus shares a final meal with his disciples. In that meal, Jesus chooses the manufactured items of bread and wine to represent himself and his coming sacrifice. Holding up a loaf of bread, he says, "This is my body" (Matt. 26:26); then holding up the skin of wine, he says, "This is my blood" (Matt. 26:28). The Son of God is the product of no one's work, not even the Father's. In the words of the Nicene Creed, he is "begotten, not made." But he chooses common, tangible things like bread and wine, made by people, to illustrate his sacrifice. As Alan Richardson puts it:

> Without the toil and skill of the farmer, without the labor of the bakers, the transport workers, the banks and offices, the shops and distributors— without, in fact, the toil of mines and shipyards and steel-works and so on—*this* loaf would not have been here to lay upon the altar this morning. In truth, the whole world of human work is involved in the manufacture of the bread and wine which we offer. . . . Here is the strange unbreakable link that exists between the bread that is won in the sweat of man's face and the bread of life that is bought without money or without price.[19]

The entire community participates.

---

[19] Alan Richardson, *The Biblical Doctrine of Work*, Ecumenical Bible Studies No. 1 (London: SCM Press for the Study Department of the World Council of Churches, 1952; repr. 1954), 70.

We cannot pretend to know why Jesus chose tangible products of human labor to represent himself rather than natural articles or abstract ideas or images of his own design. But the fact is that he *did* dignify these products of work as the representation of his own infinite dignity. When we remember that in his resurrection he also bears a physical body (Matt. 28:9, 13), there can be no room to imagine the kingdom of God as a spiritual realm divorced from the physical reality of God's creation. After creating us (Gen. 2:7; John 1), he chose articles of our handiwork to represent himself. This is a grace almost beyond comprehension.

Jesus' Death, Resurrection, and Commissioning of His Followers (Matthew 27–28)

More than any other Gospel writer, Matthew emphasizes the earth-shattering implications of the death and resurrection of Jesus Christ, and brings us back to the central motif of the kingdoms of heaven and earth. The darkening of the heavens, the shaking of the earth, and the resurrection of the dead (Matt. 27:45–54) would have been clear signs to the Jews that the present age was ending and the age to come had begun. Yet life and work seem to go on as they always had; it was business as usual. Did anything really change at that cross on Golgotha's hill?

The Gospel according to Matthew answers with a resounding yes. Jesus' crucifixion was the deathblow for a world system founded on pretensions of human power and wisdom. His resurrection marks the definitive intrusion of God's ways into the world. The reign of God's kingdom has not yet taken in the entire earth, but Christ governs all those who will follow him.

Jesus' earthly ministry was ending. Matthew 28:16–20 narrates his commissioning of those who followed him:

> Now the eleven disciples went to Galilee, to the mountain to which Jesus had directed them. When they saw him, they worshiped him; but some doubted. And Jesus came and said to them, "All authority in heaven and on earth has been given to me. Go, therefore, and make disciples of all nations, baptizing them in the name of the Father and of the Son and of the Holy Spirit, and teaching them to obey everything that I have commanded you. And remember, I am with you always, to the end of the age."

This passage is often referred to as the Great Commission, and Christians tend to focus on its evangelistic aspect. But the commission is actually to "make disciples," not merely to "win converts." As we have seen throughout this article, work is an essential element of being a disciple. Understanding our work in the context of the Lordship of Christ is part of fulfilling the Great Commission.

We have our marching orders. We are to take the good news to all nations, baptizing those who believe the good news, and teaching them "to obey everything that I have commanded you" (Matt. 26:20). As we look back over these twenty-eight chapters of Matthew, we see many commands that touch us in the workplace. These teachings are for us and for those who come after us.

Conclusion to Matthew

God cares about our work, and the Scriptures have much to say about this. As noted at the beginning, the Gospel according to Matthew addresses the theology and practice of work on many fronts: leadership and authority, power and influence, business practices, truth and deception, treatment of workers, conflict resolution, wealth and the necessities of life, workplace relationships, investing and saving, rest, and living in God's kingdom while working in secular places.

Christians often assume that our lives are to be split into two realms, the secular and the sacred. Our work can become merely a way of earning a living, a secular activity with no godly significance. Going to church and personal devotion are assumed to be the only sacred elements of life. A misreading of Matthew could support this split. The kingdom of the earth could represent the material, secular parts of life; and the kingdom of heaven, the sacred, ethereal parts. But a true reading of Matthew is that both kingdoms include all of life. The kingdom of God has both material and spiritual aspects, and so does the kingdom of the fallen earth. The Christian way is to put our entire life, including our work life, at the service of God's kingdom, which Christ is bringing to earth even now.

Jesus calls his followers to live and work in the midst of the fallen world, while holding fast to God's purposes, virtues, and principles. For individual Christians, the sacred and the secular cannot be separated: "No one can serve two masters" (Matt. 6:24). In this universe created and sustained by God, there is no "secular" space, immune to his influence, out of his control, or over which he does not claim sovereignty.

But while the kingdom of darkness remains, the kingdom of God is also at hand. The world's people and systems often do not reflect the ways of God. Those called by Christ have to learn how to serve God's kingdom faithfully, while learning to exist amid the very real powers that oppose God's way. The Christian worldview cannot be one of escape or disregard for this world. Above all people, Christians should rightly be engaged in creating structures that reflect the kingdom of God in all realms of life, the workplace included. We are to model the practices of God's kingdom in our workplaces, especially practices in which we turn over our power and wealth to God and depend on his power and provision. This is what it means to live (not just speak) the paradigmatic prayer of the Lord: "Thy kingdom come. Thy will be done, on earth as it is in heaven."

MARK AND WORK

Introduction to Mark

The Gospel of Mark, like the other Gospels, is about the work of Jesus. His work is to teach, to heal, to perform signs of God's power, and most of all to die and be raised to life for the benefit of humanity. Christ's work is absolutely unique. Yet it is also a seamless part of the work of all God's people, which is to cooperate with God in restoring the world to the way God intended it from the beginning. Our work is not Christ's work, but our work has the same end as his. Therefore the Gospel of Mark is not *about* our work, but it *informs* our work and *defines* the ultimate goal of our work.

By studying Mark, we discover God's call to work in the service of his kingdom. We discern the rhythms of work, rest, and worship God intends for our lives. We see the opportunities and dangers inherent in earning a living, accumulating wealth, gaining status, paying taxes, and working in a society that does not necessarily aim toward God's purposes. We meet fishermen, laborers, mothers and fathers (parenting is a type of work!), tax collectors, people with disabilities that affect their work, leaders, farmers, lawyers, priests, builders, philanthropists (mostly women), a very rich man, merchants, bankers, soldiers, and governors. We recognize the same bewildering range of personalities we encounter in life and work today. We encounter people not as isolated individuals, but as members of families, communities, and nations. Work and workers are everywhere in the Gospel of Mark.

Mark is the briefest Gospel. It contains less of Jesus' teaching material than Matthew and Luke. Our task, then, must be to pay close attention to the details in Mark to see how his Gospel applies to non-church work. The primary work-related passages in Mark fall into three categories: (1) call narratives, as Jesus calls disciples to work on behalf of God's kingdom; (2) Sabbath controversies concerning the rhythm of work and rest; and (3) economic issues concerning wealth and its accumulation, and taxation. We will discuss the call narratives under the heading "Kingdom and Discipleship," the Sabbath controversies under the heading "Rhythms of Work, Rest, and Worship," and the episodes related to taxation and wealth under "Economic Issues." In each of these categories, Mark is primarily concerned with how those who would follow Jesus must be transformed at a deep level.

As with the other Gospels, Mark is set against a background of turbulent economic times. During the Roman era, Galilee was undergoing major social upheaval, with land increasingly owned by a wealthy few—often foreigners—and with a general movement away from small-scale farming to larger-scale, estate-based agriculture. Those who had once been tenant farmers or even landowners were forced to become day laborers, often as a result of having lost their own property through the foreclosure of loans taken to pay Roman taxes.[1] Set against such a background, it is small wonder that economic and fiscal themes emerge in Mark's narrative and in the teaching of Jesus, and an awareness of this social context allows us to appreciate undercurrents in these that we might otherwise have overlooked.

Kingdom and Discipleship (Mark 1–4; 6; 8)

The Beginning of the Gospel (Mark 1:1–13)

The accounts of John's preaching and of Jesus' baptism and temptation say nothing directly about work. Nevertheless, as the narrative gateway to the Gospel, they provide the basic thematic context for all that follows and cannot be bypassed as we move to passages more obviously applicable to our concerns. An interesting point is that Mark's title (Mark 1:1) describes the book as "the *beginning* of the good news about Jesus Christ." From a narrative point of view, drawing attention to the beginning is striking, because the Gospel seems to lack an ending. The earliest manuscripts suggest that the Gospel ends suddenly with Mark 16:8: "So they went out and fled from the tomb, for terror and amazement had seized them; and they said nothing to anyone, for they were afraid." The

---

[1] Sean Freyne, *Jesus: A Jewish Galilean* (London: T&T Clark, 2004), 45–46.

text ends so abruptly that scribes added the material now found in Mark
16:9–20, which is composed from passages found elsewhere in the New
Testament. But perhaps Mark intended his Gospel to have no ending. It
is only "the beginning of the good news of Jesus Christ," and we who read
it are participants in the continuing Gospel. If this is so, then our lives are
a direct continuation of the events in Mark, and we have every reason to
expect concrete applications to our work.[2]

We will see in greater detail that Mark always portrays human followers of Jesus as beginners who fall far short of perfection. This is true
even of the twelve apostles. Mark, more than any of the other Gospels,
presents the apostles as unperceptive, ignorant, and repeatedly failing
Jesus. This is highly encouraging, for many Christians who try to follow Christ in their work feel inadequate in doing so. Take heart, Mark
exhorts, for in this we are like the apostles themselves!

John the Baptist (Mark 1:2–11) is presented as the messenger of Malachi 3:1 and Isaiah 40:3. He announces the coming of "the Lord." Combined with the designation of Jesus as "Christ, the Son of God" (Mark
1:1), this language makes clear to the reader that Mark's central theme is
"the kingdom of God," even though he waits until Mark 1:15 to use that
phrase and to connect it to the gospel ("good news"). "The kingdom of
God" is not a geographical concept in Mark. It is the reign of the Lord
observed as people and peoples come under God's rule, through the
transforming work of the Spirit. That work is highlighted by Mark's brief
description of the baptism and temptation of Jesus (Mark 1:9–13), which
by its brevity emphasizes the descent of the Spirit onto Jesus and his role
in driving him into (and presumably through) the temptation by Satan.

This passage cuts across two opposite, yet popular, conceptions of the
kingdom of God. On the one hand is the idea that the kingdom of God does
not yet exist, and will not until Christ returns to rule the world in person.
Under this view, the workplace, like the rest of the world, is enemy territory.
The Christian's duty is to survive in the enemy territory of this world long
enough to evangelize, and profitably enough to meet personal needs and
give money to the church. The other is the idea that the kingdom of God is
an inner, spiritual domain, having nothing to do with the world around us.

---

[2] J. David Hester, "Dramatic Inconclusion: Irony and the Narrative Rhetoric of
the Ending of Mark," *Journal for the Study of the New Testament* 17 (1995): 61–86.

Under this view, what the Christian does at work, or anywhere else aside from church and individual prayer time, is of no concern to God at all.

Against both of these ideas, Mark makes it clear that Jesus' coming inaugurates the kingdom of God as a present reality on earth. Jesus says plainly, "The time is fulfilled, and the kingdom of God has come near; repent, and believe in the good news" (Mark 1:15). The kingdom is not fulfilled at present, of course. It does not yet govern the earth, and will not do so until Christ returns. But it is here now, and it is real.

Therefore, to submit to the reign of God and to proclaim his kingdom has very real consequences in the world around us. It may well bring us into social disrepute, conflict, and, indeed, suffering. Mark 1:14, like Matthew 4:12, draws attention to John's imprisonment and links this to the commencement of Jesus' own proclamation that "the kingdom has come near" (Mark 1:15). The kingdom is thus set over against the powers of the world, and as readers we are forcefully shown that to serve the gospel and to honor God will not necessarily bring success in this life. Yet at the same time, by the Spirit's power, Christians are called to serve God for the benefit of those around them, as the healings Jesus performs demonstrate (Mark 1:23–34, 40–45).

The radical significance of the Holy Spirit's coming into the world is made clearer later in the Gospel through the Beelzebul controversy (Mark 3:20–30). This is a difficult section, and we have to be quite careful in how we deal with it, but it is certainly not unimportant to the theology of the kingdom that undergirds our theology of work. The logic of the passage seems to be that by casting out demons, Jesus is effectively liberating the world from Satan, depicted as a strong man now bound. Like their Lord, Christians are meant to employ the Spirit's power to transform the world, not to escape the world or to accommodate to it.

The Calling of the First Disciples (Mark 1:16–20)

This section needs to be treated cautiously: while the disciples are paradigms of the Christian life, they also occupy a unique position in the story of salvation. Their summons to a distinctive kind of service, and to the forsaking of their current employment, does not establish a universal pattern for Christian life and vocation. Many, indeed most, of those who follow Jesus do not quit their jobs to do so. Nevertheless, the way in which the demands of the kingdom cut across and override the usual principles of society is transferable and enlightening to our work.

The opening clause of Mark 1:16 presents Jesus as itinerant ("as he passed along"), and he calls these fishermen to follow him on the road. This is more than just a challenge to leave behind income and stability or, as we might put it, to get out of our "comfort zone." Mark's account of this incident records a detail lacking in the other accounts, namely, that James and John leave their father Zebedee "with the hired men" (Mark 1:20). They themselves were not hired men or day laborers, but rather were a part of what was probably a relatively successful family business. As Suzanne Watts Henderson notes in relation to the response of the disciples, the "piling up of particulars underscores the full weight of the verb [to leave]: not just nets are left behind, but a named father, a boat and indeed an entire enterprise."[3] For these disciples to follow Jesus, they have to demonstrate a willingness to allow their identity, status, and worth to be determined primarily in relation to him.

Fishing was a major industry in Galilee, with a connected sub-industry of fish salting.[4] At a time of social turbulence in Galilee, these two related industries supported each other and remained steady. The willingness of the disciples to forsake such stability is quite remarkable. Economic stability is no longer their chief purpose for working. Yet even here we must be cautious. Jesus does not reject the earthly vocation of these men but reorients it. Jesus calls Simon and Andrew to be "fishers of people" (Mark 1:17), thereby affirming their former work as an image of the new role to which he is calling them. Although most Christians are not called to leave their jobs and become wandering preachers, we are called to ground our identity in Christ. Whether we leave our jobs or not, a disciple's identity is no longer "fisherman," "tax collector," or anything else except "follower of Jesus." This challenges us to resist the temptation to make our work the defining element of our sense of who we are.

---

[3] Suzanne Watts Henderson, *Christology and Discipleship in the Gospel of Mark* (Cambridge: Cambridge University Press, 2006), 63.

[4] Freyne, 48–53. For the place of fishing in the taxation structures, see Bruce Malina and Richard Rohrbaugh, *A Social-Scientific Commentary on the Synoptic Gospels* (Minneapolis: Fortress Press, 1992), 44–45.

The Paralytic Man (Mark 2:1–12)

The story of Jesus healing the paralytic man raises the question of what the theology of work means for those who do not have the ability to work. The paralytic man, prior to this healing, is incapable of self-supporting work. As such, he is dependent on the grace and compassion of those around him for his daily survival. Jesus is impressed by the faith of the man's friends. Their faith is active, showing care, compassion, and friendship to someone who was excluded from both the financial and relational rewards of work. In their faith, there is no separation between being and doing.

Jesus sees their effort as an act of collective faith. "When Jesus saw *their* faith, he said to the paralytic, 'Son, your sins are forgiven'" (Mark 2:5). Regrettably, the *community* of faith plays a vanishingly small role in most Christians' work lives in the modern West. Even if we receive help and encouragement for the workplace from our church, it is almost certain to be *individual* help and encouragement. In earlier times, most Christians worked alongside the same people they went to church with, so churches could easily apply the Scriptures to the shared occupations of laborers, farmers, and householders. In contrast, Western Christians today seldom work in the same locations as others in the same church. Nonetheless, today's Christians often work in the same *types* of jobs as others in their faith communities. So there could be an opportunity to share their work challenges and opportunities with other believers in similar occupations. Yet this seldom happens. Unless we find a way for *groups* of Christian workers to support one another, grow together, and develop some kind of work-related Christian community, we miss out on the communal nature of faith that is so essential in Mark 2:3–12.

In this brief episode, then, we observe three things: (1) Work is intended to benefit those who can't support themselves through work, as well as those who can; (2) faith and work are not separated as being and doing, but are integrated into action empowered by God; and (3) work done in faith cries out for a community of faith to support it.

The Calling of Levi (Mark 2:13–17)

The calling of Levi is another incident that occurs as Jesus is moving (Mark 2:13–14). The passage stresses the public nature of this summons.

Jesus calls Levi while teaching a crowd (Mark 2:14), and Levi is initially seen "sitting at the tax booth." His employment would make him a figure of contempt for many of his Galilean contemporaries. There is a measure of debate over just how heavily Roman and Herodian taxation was felt in Galilee, but most think that the issue was rather sore. The actual collection of taxes was contracted out to private tax collectors. A tax collector paid the tax for his entire territory upfront, and collected the individual taxes from the populace later. To make this profitable, he had to charge the populace more than the actual tax rate and the tax collector pocketed the mark-up. The Roman authorities thereby delegated the politically sensitive work of tax collection to members of the local community, but it led to a high rate of effective tax, and it opened the doors to all sorts of corruption.[5] It is likely that this was one of the factors contributing to land loss in Galilee, as landowners took loans to pay monetary taxes and then, if their harvests were poor, lost their properties as collateral. The fact that we initially encounter Levi in his tax booth means that he is, in effect, a living symbol of Roman occupation and a reminder of the fact that some Jews were willing collaborators with the Romans. The link made in Mark 2:16 between tax collectors and "sinners" reinforces the negative associations.[6]

Where Luke stresses that Levi leaves everything to answer Jesus' call (Luke 5:28), Mark simply recounts that Levi follows him. The tax collector then throws a banquet, opening his house to Jesus, his disciples, and a mixed group including other tax collectors and "sinners." While the image is suggestive of a man seeking to share the gospel with his business colleagues, the reality is probably a little more subtle. Levi's "community" comprises his colleagues and others who, as "sinners," are shunned by leading figures in the community. In other words, their work made them part of a sub-community that had high-quality social relationships internally, but low-quality relationships with the communities around them. This is true for many kinds of work today. Our co-workers may be much more open to us than our neighbors are. Being a member of a work community may help us facilitate an encounter with the reality of the gospel for our co-workers.

---

[5] Malina and Rohrbaugh, 189–90.

[6] The Mishnaic text *m. Toharot* 7:6 states that if a tax collector enters a house, then it becomes unclean.

Interestingly, the hospitality of communal eating is a major part of Jesus' ministry and suggests a concrete way by which such encounters might be hosted. The hospitality of lunch with colleagues, a jog or workout at the gym, or a shared beverage after work can build deeper relationships with our co-workers. These friendships have lasting value themselves, and through them the Holy Spirit may open the door to a kind of friendship evangelism.

This raises a question. If Christians today were to host a meal with colleagues from work, friends from their neighborhood, and friends from their church, what would they talk about? The Christian faith has much to say about how to be a good worker and how to be a good neighbor. But do Christians know how to speak about them in a common language understandable to their colleagues and neighbors? If the conversation turned to workplace or civic topics such as a job search, customer service, property taxes, or zoning, would we be able to speak meaningfully to nonbelievers about how Christian concepts apply to such issues? Do our churches equip us for these conversations? It appears that Levi—or Jesus—was able to speak meaningfully about how Jesus' message applied to the lives of the people gathered there. (The question of taxation will recur later in the Gospel and we defer until then some of our questions about Jesus' attitude toward it.)

The Twelve (Mark 3:13–19)

In addition to the accounts of the calling of specific disciples, there is also the account of the appointing of the apostles. There is an important point to be noted in Mark 3:13–14, namely, that the Twelve constitute a special group within the broader community of disciples. The uniqueness of their apostolic office is important. They are called to a distinctive form of service, one that may depart significantly from the experience most of us will have. If we are to draw lessons from the experience and roles of the disciples, then it must be through recognition of how their actions and convictions relate to the kingdom, not merely the fact that they left their jobs to follow Jesus.

The qualifications listed for Simon, James, John, and Judas in Mark 3:16–19 are relevant here. Simon's name is, of course, supplemented with the new name given to him by Jesus, "Peter," which closely resembles the Greek word for "rock" (*petros*). One cannot help but wonder if there is both a certain irony and a certain promise in the name. Simon, as fickle and unstable as he will prove to be, is named The Rock, and one day he will live up to that name. Like him, our service to God in our workplaces, just as elsewhere in our lives, will not be a matter of instantaneous perfection, but rather one of failure and growth. This is a helpful thought at times when we feel we have failed and brought the kingdom into disrepute in the process.

Just as Simon is given a new name, so too are the sons of Zebedee, referred to as the "Sons of Thunder" (Mark 3:17). It is a quirky nickname, and seems humorous, but it also quite likely picks up on the character or personality of these two men.[7] It is an interesting point that personality and personality types are not effaced by inclusion in the kingdom. This cuts both ways. On one hand, our personalities continue to be part of our identity in the kingdom, and our embodiment of the kingdom in our place of work continues to be mediated through that personality. The temptation to find our identity in some stereotype, even a Christian one, is challenged by this. Yet, at the same time, our personalities may be marked by elements that themselves ought to be challenged by the gospel. There is a hint of this in the title given to Zebedee's sons, since it suggests a short temper or a tendency toward conflict and, even though the name is given with fondness, it may not be a nickname to be proud of.

The issue of personality makes a significant contribution to our understanding of applying the Christian faith to our work. Most of us would probably say that our experiences of work, both good and bad, have been greatly affected by the personalities of those around us. Often the very character qualities that make someone an inspiring and energizing colleague can make that person a difficult one. A motivated and excited worker might be easily distracted by new projects, or might be prone to quickly formed (and quickly expressed) opinions. Our own personality plays a huge role too. We may find others easy to work with or difficult, based as much on our personalities as theirs. Likewise, others may find *us* easy or difficult to work with.

But it is more than a matter of getting along with others easily. Our distinctive personalities shape our abilities to contribute to our organization's work—and through it to the work of God's kingdom—for better or worse. Personality gives us both strengths and weaknesses. To a certain degree, following Christ means allowing him to curb the

---

[7] Robert. A. Guelich, *Mark 1–8:26*, vol. 34A, *Word Biblical Commentary* (Nashville: Thomas Nelson, 1989), 162.

excesses of our personality, as when he rebuked the Sons of Thunder for their misguided ambition to sit at his right and left hands (Mark 10:35–45). At the same time, Christians often err by setting up particular personality traits as a universal model. Some Christian communities have privileged traits such as extraversion, mildness, reticence to use power, or—more darkly—abusiveness, intolerance, and gullibility. Some Christians find that the traits that make them good at their jobs—decisiveness, skepticism about dogma, or ambition, for example—make them feel guilty or marginalized in church. Trying to be something we are not, in the sense of trying to fit a stereotype of what a Christian in the workplace ought to be like, can be highly problematic and can leave others feeling that we are inauthentic. We may be called to imitate Christ (Phil. 2:5) and our leaders (Heb. 13:7), but this is a matter of emulating virtue, not personality. Jesus, in any case, chose people with a variety of personalities as his friends and workers. Many tools are available to help individuals and organizations make better use of the variety of personality characteristics with respect to decision making, career choice, group performance, conflict resolution, leadership, relationships at work, and other factors.

While on one level this needs to be related to a theology of wealth or property, on another level it needs to be related to the point at which the theologies of church and work meet. It is always tempting, and in fact can seem like an obligation, to maintain a network of Christians within the working environment and to seek to support one another. While laudable, there needs to be a certain reality injected into this. Some of those who present themselves as followers of Jesus may, in fact, have misplaced hearts, and this may affect the opinions they advocate. At such times, our responsibility as Christians is to be prepared to challenge one another in love, to hold one another to account as to whether we are truly operating according to the standards of the kingdom.

Discipleship in Process (Mark 4:35–41; 6:45–52; 8:14–21)

The Gospel of Mark, more than the other Gospels, highlights the ignorance, weakness, and selfishness of the disciples. This comes despite the many good things Mark has to say about them, including their response to Jesus' initial call (Mark 1:16–20) and to his commissioning of them (Mark 6:7–13).[8]

Certain incidents and narrative devices develop this portrait. One is the repetition of boat scenes (Mark 4:35–41; 6:45–52; 8:14–21), which parallel one another in emphasizing the disciples' inability to truly comprehend Jesus' power and authority. The last boat scene is closely followed by the unusual two-stage healing of a blind man (Mark 8:22–26), which may function as a kind of narrative metaphor for the only partial vision of the disciples regarding Jesus.[9] Then follows Peter's confession of Christ (Mark 8:27–33), with his dramatic moment of insight followed immediately by Satanic blindness on the apostle's part. The disciples' limited grasp of Jesus' identity is matched by their limited grasp of his message. They continue to desire power and status (Mark 9:33–37; 10:13–16; 10:35–45). Jesus challenges them several times for their failure to recognize that following him requires a fundamental attitude of self-sacrifice. Most obviously, of course, the disciples desert Jesus at the time of his arrest and trial (Mark 14:50–51). The juxtaposition of Peter's threefold denial (Mark 14:66–72) with the death of Jesus throws the cowardice and courage of the two men, respectively, into sharper relief.

Yet Peter and the others will go on to lead the church effectively. The angel who speaks to the women following the resurrection (Mark 16:6–7) gives them a message to the disciples (and Peter is singled out!), promising a further encounter with the resurrected Jesus. The disciples will be very different following this encounter, a fact that Mark does not explore but that is well developed in Acts, so that the resurrection is the key event in effecting such change.

What relevance does this have to work? Simply and obviously, that as disciples of Jesus with our own work to do, we are imperfect and in process. There will be a good deal that we will be required to repent of, attitudes that will be wrong and will need to change. Significantly, we must recognize that, like the disciples, we may well be wrong in much of what we believe and think, even about gospel matters. On a daily level, then, we must prayerfully reflect on how we are embodying the reign of God and prepare to

---

[8] Henderson, *in toto*.
[9] Guelich, 426.

show repentance over our deficiencies in this regard. We may feel tempted to portray ourselves as righteous, wise, and skilled in our workplaces, as a witness to Jesus' righteousness, wisdom, and excellence. But it would be a more honest and more powerful witness to portray ourselves as we really are—fallible and somewhat self-centered works-in-process, evidence of Jesus' mercy more than demonstrators of his character. Our witness is then to invite our co-workers to grow along with us in the ways of God, rather than to become like us. Of course, we need to exercise ourselves rigorously to growth in Christ. God's mercy is not an excuse to be complacent in our sin.

Rhythms of Work, Rest, and Worship (Mark 1–4; 6; 13)

The First Days of the Movement (Mark 1:21–45)

A major block of material (Mark 1:21–34) takes place on the Sabbath, the day of rest. Within this block, some of the action is located in the synagogue (Mark 1:21–28). It is significant that the weekly routine of work, rest, and worship is integrated into Jesus' own life and is neither ignored nor discarded. In our own age, where such a practice has been greatly diminished, it is important to remind ourselves that this weekly rhythm was endorsed by Jesus. Of course, it is also significant that Jesus does his work of both truth and healing on this day. This will later bring him into conflict with the Pharisees. It also highlights that the Sabbath is not just a day of rest from work, but also a day of active love and mercy.[10]

As well as the weekly rhythm, there is also a daily rhythm. Following the Sabbath, Jesus rises while it is still "very dark" to pray (Mark 1:35). His first priority of the day is to connect with God. The emphasis on the solitude of Jesus in this time of prayer is important, stressing that this prayer is not a public performance, but a matter of personal communion.

Daily prayer seems to be an extremely difficult practice for many workplace Christians. Between early morning family responsibili-

---

[10] David Shepherd, *Seeking Sabbath: A Personal Journey* (Oxford: Bible Reading Fellowship, 2007) is a helpful and thought-provoking reflection on the significance of the Sabbath for the contemporary world and highly recommended for further reading.

ties, long commutes, early working hours, a desire to get ahead of the day's responsibilities, and late nights needed to accomplish the day's work (or entertainment), it seems almost impossible to establish a consistent routine of morning prayer. And later in the day is harder still. Nowhere does Mark depict judgment against those who do not or cannot pray daily about the work that lies ahead of them. But he does depict Jesus—busier than anyone around him—praying about the work and the people God sets before him every day. Amid the pressures of working life, daily prayer may seem to be a personal luxury we can't afford to indulge. Jesus, however, couldn't imagine going to his work without prayer, much as most of us couldn't imagine going to work without shoes.

Regular time set apart for prayer is a good thing, but it is not the only way to pray. We can also pray in the midst of our work. One practice many have found helpful is to pray very briefly at multiple times during the day. "Daily Devotions for Individuals and Families," found in the Book of Common Prayer (pages 136–143), provides brief structures for prayer in the morning, at noon, in the later afternoon and at night, taking account of the rhythms of life and work during the day. Even briefer examples include a one- or two-sentence prayer when moving from one task to another, praying with eyes open, offering thanks silently or out loud before meals, keeping an object or verse of Scripture in a pocket as a reminder to pray and many others. Among the many books that help establish a daily prayer rhythm are *Finding God in the Fast Lane* by Joyce Huggett[11] and *The Spirit of the Disciplines* by Dallas Willard.[12]

The Lord of the Sabbath (Mark 2:23–3:6)

We have noticed already, in our discussion of Mark 1:21–34, that the Sabbath is integrated into the weekly rhythm of Jesus' life. The clash that takes place between Jesus and the Pharisees is not over whether to observe the Sabbath but over *how* to observe it. For the Pharisees, the Sabbath was primarily defined in negative terms. What,

---

[11] Joyce Huggett, *Finding God in the Fast Lane* (Suffolk, UK: Kevin Mayhew, 2004).

[12] Dallas Willard, *The Spirit of the Disciplines: Understanding How God Changes Lives* (San Francisco: Harper and Row, 1988).

they would ask, is prohibited by the commandment to do no work (Exod. 20:8–11; Deut. 5:12–15)?[13] To them, even the casual action of the disciples in picking ears of grain constitutes a kind of work and thus ignores the prohibition. It is interesting that they describe this action as "not lawful" (Mark 2:24), even though such a specific application of the fourth commandment is lacking in the Torah. They regard their own interpretation of the law as authoritative and binding, and do not consider the possibility that they might be wrong. Even more objectionable for them is Jesus' act of healing (Mark 3:1–6), which is depicted as the key event leading the Pharisees to plot against Jesus.

In contrast to the Pharisees, Jesus regards the Sabbath positively. The day of freedom from work is a gift for humanity's good: "The sabbath was made for humankind, not humankind for the sabbath" (Mark 2:27). Moreover, the Sabbath affords opportunities to exercise compassion and love. Such a view of the Sabbath has good prophetic antecedent. Isaiah 58 links the Sabbath with compassion and social justice in the service of God, culminating with a description of God's blessing on those who will "call the sabbath a delight" (Isa. 58:13–14). The juxtaposition of compassion, justice, and Sabbath suggests that the Sabbath is most fully used as a day of worship by the demonstration of compassion and justice. After all, the Sabbath itself is a remembrance of God's justice and compassion in delivering Israel from slavery in Egypt (Deut. 5:15).

The first Sabbath account (Mark 2:23–28) is triggered by the disciples' action of picking ears of grain.[14] While Matthew adds that the disciples were hungry, and Luke describes their action of rubbing the ears of grain between their hands before eating them, Mark simply describes them as picking the grain, which conveys the casual nature of the action. The disciples were probably absently picking at the seeds and nibbling them. The defense that Jesus offers when challenged by the Pharisees seems a little strange at first, because it is a story about the temple, not the Sabbath.

---

[13] Rabbinic traditions on this point are widespread. Most obviously, see *m. Sabb.* 7:2 and *m. Besah* 5:2.

[14] Lutz Doering, "Sabbath Laws in the New Testament Gospels," in *The New Testament and Rabbinic Literature*, ed. F. García Martínez and P. J. Tomson (Leiden: Brill, 2009), 208–20.

"Have you never read what David did when he and his companions were hungry and in need of food? He entered the house of God, when Abiathar was high priest, and ate the bread of the Presence, which it is not lawful for any but the priests to eat, and he gave some to his companions." (Mark 2:25–26)

Scholars are divided over how—or even whether—Jesus' argument works according to principles of Jewish exegesis and argumentation.[15] The key is to recognize the concept of "holiness." Both the Sabbath and the temple (with its contents) are described as "holy" in Scripture.[16] Sabbath is sacred time, the temple is sacred space, but lessons that may be derived from the holiness of one may be transferred to the other.

Jesus' point is that the holiness of the temple does not preclude its participation in acts of compassion and justice. The sacred spaces of earth are not refuges of holiness *against* the world, but places of God's presence *for* the world, for his sustenance and restoration of the world. A place set apart for God fundamentally *is* a place of justice and compassion. "The sabbath [and by implication, the temple] was made for humankind, and not humankind for the sabbath" (Mark 2:27). Matthew's version of this account includes the detail, "I desire mercy and not sacrifice," from Hosea 6:6 (Matt. 12:7). This makes explicit the point that we see with more reserve in Mark.

The same point emerges in the second Sabbath controversy, when Jesus heals a man in a synagogue on the Sabbath (Mark 3:1–6). The key question that Jesus asks is, "Is it lawful to do good or to do harm on the Sabbath, to save life or to kill?" The silence of the Pharisees in the face of this question serves as a confirmation that the Sabbath is honored by doing good, by saving life.

How does this apply to our work today? The Sabbath principle is that we must consecrate a portion of our time and keep it free from the demands of work, allowing it to take on a distinctive character of worship. This is not

---

[15] Guelich, 121–30.

[16] The Sabbath is referred to as holy in Exodus 31:14–15, picking up on the command in the Decalogue to "keep it holy" (Exod. 20:8), recognizing that God himself has "consecrated" it (Exod. 20:11). This notion of holiness links the Sabbath to the temple, which is characteristically understood as "holy" (see, for example, Ps. 5:7 or Ps. 11:4) and, of course, has at its heart the "Holy of Holies."

to say that the Sabbath is the only time of worship, nor that work cannot be a form of worship itself. But the Sabbath principle allows us time to focus on God in a different way than the working week allows, and to enjoy his blessing in a distinctive way. Crucially, too, it gives us space to allow our worship of God to manifest itself in social compassion, care, and love. Our worship on the Sabbath flavors our work during the week.

Recognizing that there is no single Christian perspective about the Sabbath, the Theology of Work Project explores a somewhat different point of view in the section on "Sabbath and Work" in the chapter "Luke and Work."

Jesus the Builder (Mark 6:1–6)

An incident in Jesus' hometown gives a rare insight into his work prior to becoming a traveling preacher. The context is that Jesus' hometown friends and acquaintances can't believe that this familiar local boy has become a great teacher and prophet. In the course of their complaints, they say, "What deeds of power are being done by his hands! Is not this the carpenter, the son of Mary and brother of James and Joses and Judas and Simon, and are not his sisters here with us?" (Mark 6:2–3). This is the only passage in the Bible to directly state Jesus' trade. (In Matthew 13:55, Jesus is called "the carpenter's son," and Luke and John do not mention his profession.) The under-lying Greek (*tekton*) refers to a builder or craftsman in any kind of material,[17] which in Palestine would generally be stone or brick. The English rendering "carpenter" may reflect the fact that in London wood was the more common building material at the time the first English translations were made.

In any case, a number of Jesus' parables take place at construction sites. How much of Jesus' personal experience might be reflected in these parables? Did he help construct a fence, dig a wine press, or build a tower in a vineyard, and observe the strained relations between the landowner and the tenants (Mark 12:1–12)? Did one of his customers run out of money halfway through building a tower and leave an unpaid

---

[17] Ken M. Campbell, "What was Jesus' Occupation?" *Journal of the Evangelical Theological Society* 48, no. 3 (September 2005): 501–19.

debt to Jesus (Luke 14:28–30)? Did he remember Joseph teaching him how to dig a foundation all the way to solid rock, so that the building can withstand wind and flood (Matt. 7:24–27)? Did he ever hire assistants and have to face grumbling about pay (Matt. 20:1–16) and pecking order (Mark 9:33–37)? Was he ever supervised by a manager who asked him to join in a scheme to defraud the owner (Luke 16:1–16)? In short, how much of the wisdom in Jesus' parables was developed through his experience as a tradesman in the first-century economy? If nothing else, remembering Jesus' experience as a builder can help us see the parables in a more concrete light.

Parables at Work (Mark 4:26–29 and 13:32–37)

Mark contains only two parables that are not also found in the other Gospels. Both of them concern work, and both are very short.

The first of these parables, in Mark 4:26–29, compares the kingdom of God to growing grain from seed. It has similarities to the more familiar parable of the mustard seed, which follows immediately afterwards, and to the parable of the sower (Mark 4:1–8). Although the parable is set in the workplace of agriculture, the role of the farmer is deliberately minimized. "He does not know how" the grain grows (Mark 4:27). Instead, the emphasis is on how the kingdom's growth is brought about by the inexplicable power of God. Nonetheless, the farmer must "rise night and day" to cultivate the crop (Mark 4:26) and go in with his sickle (Mark 4:28) to reap the harvest. God's miracle is given among those who do their assigned work.

The second uniquely Marcan parable, in Mark 13:32–37, illustrates the need for Jesus' disciples to watch for his second coming. Intriguingly, Jesus says, "It is like a man going on a journey, when he leaves home and puts his slaves in charge, each with his work, and commands the doorkeeper to be on the watch" (Mark 13:34). While he is away, each servant is charged to keep doing his work. The kingdom is not like a master who goes to a far country and promises to eventually call his servants to join him there. No, the master will be coming back, and he gives his servants the work of growing and maintaining his household for his eventual return.

Both parables take it as a given that Jesus' disciples are diligent workers, whatever their occupation. We will not discuss the other parables here, but refer instead to the extensive explorations in "Matthew and Work" and "Luke and Work."

Economic Issues (Mark 10–12)

The Rich Young Man and Attitudes to Wealth and Status (Mark 10:17–31)

Wealth (Mark 10:17–22)

Jesus' encounter with a rich man who asks "What must I do to inherit eternal life?" constitutes one of the few passages in Mark that speaks directly to economic activity. The man's question leads Jesus to list (Mark 10:18) the six most socially oriented commandments in the Decalogue. Interestingly, "Do not covet" (Exod. 20:17; Deut. 5:21) is presented with a definite commercial twist as "Do not defraud." The rich man says that he has "kept all of these since my youth" (Mark 10:20). But Jesus states that the one thing he lacks is treasure in heaven, obtained by sacrificing his earthly wealth and following the vagrant from Galilee. This presents an obstacle that the rich man cannot pass. It seems that he loves the comforts and security afforded by his possessions too much. Mark 10:22 emphasizes the affective dimension of the situation: "When he heard this, he was shocked and went away grieving." The young man is emotionally disturbed by Jesus' teaching, indicating an openness to its truth, but he is not able to follow through. His emotional attachment to his wealth and status overrules his willingness to heed the words of Jesus.

Applying this to work today requires real sensitivity and honesty with regard to our own instincts and values. Wealth is sometimes a *result* of work—ours or someone else's—but *work itself* can also be an emotional obstacle to following Jesus. If we have privileged positions—as the rich man did—managing our careers may become more important than serving others, doing good work, or even making time for family, civic, and spiritual life. It may hinder us from opening ourselves to an unexpected calling from God. Our wealth and privilege may make us arrogant or insensitive to the people around us. These difficulties are not unique to people of wealth and privilege, of course. Yes, Jesus' encounter with the rich man highlights that it is hard to motivate yourself to change the world if you are already on top of the heap. Before those of us of modest means and status in the Western world let ourselves off the hook, let us ask whether, by world standards, we also have become complacent because of our (relative) wealth and status.

Before we leave this episode, one crucial aspect remains. "Jesus, looking at him, loved him" (Mark 10:21). Jesus' purpose is not to shame or browbeat the young man, but to love him. He calls him to leave his possessions first of all for his *own* benefit, saying, "You will have treasure in heaven; then come, follow me." *We* are the ones who suffer when we let wealth or work cut us off from other people and remove us from relationship with God. The solution is not to try harder to be good, but to accept God's love; that is, to follow Christ. If we do this, we learn that we can trust God for the things we really need in life, and we don't need to hold on to our possessions and positions for security. (This parable is further discussed under "Luke 18:18–30" in "Luke and Work.")

Status (Mark 10:13–16, 22)

A distinctive aspect to Mark's rendering of the story is its juxtaposition with the account of the little children being brought to Jesus, and the subsequent statement that the kingdom is to be received like such infants (Mark 10:13–16). What links the two passages is probably not the issue of security, of relying on financial resources rather than on God. Rather, the point of contact is the issue of status. In ancient Mediterranean society, children were without status, or at least were of a low status.[18] They possessed none of the properties by which status was judged. Crucially, they owned nothing. The rich young man, by contrast, has an abundance of status symbols (Mark 10:22) and he owns much. (In Luke's account, he is explicitly called a "ruler," Luke 18:18.) The rich

---

[18] Malina and Rohrbaugh, 238. "Children had little status within the community or family. A minor child was on a par with a slave and only after reaching maturity was he/she a free person who could inherit the family estate. The term 'child/children' could also be used as a serious insult (see Matthew 11:16–17)."

young man may miss entering the kingdom of God as much because of his slavery to status as because of his slavery to wealth per se.

In today's workplaces, status and wealth may or may not go hand in hand. For those who grow in both wealth and status through their work, this is a double caution. Even if we manage to use wealth in a godly manner, it may prove much harder to escape the trap of slavery to status. Recently a group of billionaires received much publicity for pledging to give away at least half of their wealth.[19] Their generosity is astounding, and in no way do we wish to criticize any of the pledgers. Yet we might wonder, with the value of giving so recognized, why not give away much more than half? Half a billion dollars still exceeds by far any amount needed for a very comfortable life. Is it possible that the status of remaining a billionaire (or at least a half-billionaire) is an impediment to devoting an entire fortune to the purposes that are so clearly important to a donor? Is it any different for workers of more modest means? Does regard for status keep us from devoting more of our time, talent, and treasure to the things we recognize as truly important?

The same question can be asked of people whose status does not correlate with wealth. Academics, politicians, pastors, artists, and many others may gain great status through their work without necessarily making a lot of money. Status may arise from working, say, at a particular university or remaining the toast of a certain circle. Can that status become a form of slavery that keeps us from jeopardizing our position by taking an unpopular stance or moving on to more fruitful work elsewhere?

How painful might it be to put our work-related status at risk—even a little bit—in order to serve another person, diminish an injustice, maintain your moral integrity, or see yourself in God's eyes? Jesus had all this status and even more. Perhaps that's why he worked so hard to set aside his status through daily prayer to his Father and by putting himself constantly in disreputable company.

The Grace of God (Mark 10:23–31)

The subsequent words of Jesus (Mark 10:23–25) elaborate the significance of the encounter, as Jesus stresses the difficulty faced by the wealthy in entering the kingdom. The young man's reaction illustrates

---

[19] Stephanie Strom, "Pledge to Give Away Half Gains Billionaire Adherents," *New York Times*, August 4, 2010.

the attachment the rich have to their wealth and to the status that goes with it; significantly, the disciples themselves are "perplexed" by Jesus' statements about the wealthy. It is perhaps noteworthy that when he repeats his statement in Mark 10:24, he addresses the disciples as "children," declaring them unburdened by status. They have already been unburdened by wealth as a result of following him.

Jesus' analogy of the camel and the eye of the needle (Mark 10:25) probably has nothing to do with a small gate in Jerusalem,[20] but could be a pun on the similarity of the Greek word for a camel (*kamelos*) and that for a heavy rope (*kamilos*). The deliberately absurd image simply emphasizes the impossibility of the rich being saved without divine help. This applies to the poor as well, for otherwise "who can be saved?" (Mark 10:26). The promise of such divine help is spelled out in Mark 10:27: "For mortals it is impossible, but not for God; for God all things are possible." This keeps the passage (and hopefully us, as readers) from descending into a simple cynicism toward the rich.

This leads Peter to defend the disciples' attitudes and history of self-denial. They have "left everything" to follow Jesus. Jesus' reply affirms the heavenly reward that awaits all those who make such sacrifices. Again, the things left by such people ("house or brothers or sisters or mother or father or children or fields") potentially have connotations of status and not merely material abundance. In fact, Mark 10:31 pulls the whole account together with a forceful emphasis on status: "Many who are first will be last, and the last will be first." Up until this point, the account could reflect either a love for things in and of themselves, or for the status that those things provide. This last statement, though, places the emphasis firmly upon the issue of status. Soon after, Jesus declares this in explicit workplace terms: "Whoever wishes to become great among you must be your servant, and whoever wishes to be first among you must be slave of all" (Mark 10:44). A slave, after all, is simply a worker with no status, not even the status of owning their own ability to work. The proper status

---

[20] This is simply a myth that has circulated in popular Christian circles. William Barclay popularized it in his Daily Study Bible Commentary; see William Barclay, *The Gospel of Matthew* (Louisville, KY: Westminster John Knox Press, 2001), 253. It is unclear what the origins of this myth are, but no such gate has ever been found, in Jerusalem or elsewhere.

of Jesus' followers is that of a child or slave—no status at all. Even if we hold high positions or bear authority, we are to regard the position and authority as belonging to God, not ourselves. We are simply God's slaves, representing him but not assuming the status that belongs to him alone.

The Temple Incident (Mark 11:15–18)

The incident where Jesus drives out the vendors and moneychangers from the temple has mercantile overtones. There is a debate over the precise significance of this action, both in terms of the individual Gospel accounts and in terms of the Historical Jesus tradition.[21] Certainly, Jesus aggressively drives out those who are engaging in trade in the temple courts, whether selling clean animals and birds for sacrifice or exchanging appropriate coinage for temple offerings. It has been suggested that this is a protest over the extortionate rates being charged by those involved in the trade, and thus the abuse of the poor as they come to make offerings.[22] Alternatively, it has been seen as a rejection of the annual half-shekel temple tax.[23] Finally, it has been interpreted as a prophetic sign act, disrupting the processes of the temple as a foreshadowing of its coming destruction.[24]

Assuming we equate the temple to the church in today's environment, the incident is mostly outside our scope, which is non-church-related work. We can note, though, that the incident does cast a dim light on those who would attempt to use the church to secure workplace advantages for themselves. To join or use a church in order to gain a favored business position is both commercially damaging for the community and

---

[21] N.T. Wright, *Jesus and the Victory of God* (London: SPCK, 1996), 413–28; and more recently, J. Klawans, *Purity, Sacrifice, and the Temple: Symbolism and Supersessionism in the Study of Ancient Judaism* (New York: Oxford University Press, 2005), 213–45.

[22] Craig A. Evans, "Jesus' Action in the Temple," in *Jesus in Context: Temple, Purity, and Restoration*, ed. C. A. Evans and B. Chilton (Leiden: Brill, 1997), 395–440, esp. 419–28. Evans surveys various strands of evidence that the priests were widely regarded as greedy and corrupt. His argument is set in opposition to E. P. Sanders, *Jesus and Judaism* (Philadelphia: Fortress, 1985), 61–76. Evans's arguments are, in turn, challenged by Klawans, *Purity, Sacrifice, and the Temple*, 225–29.

[23] R. J. Bauckham, "Jesus' Demonstration in the Temple," in *Law and Religion: Essays on the Place of the Law in Israel and Early Christianity*, ed. B. Lindars (Cambridge: James Clarke, 1988), 72–89, esp. 73–74.

[24] Wright, 413–28; Sanders, 61–76.

spiritually damaging for the individual. By no means do we mean that churches and their members should avoid helping each other become better workers. But if the church becomes a commercial tool, its integrity is damaged and its witness clouded.

Taxes and Caesar (Mark 12:13–17)

The issue of taxation has arisen obliquely already, in the discussion of the call narrative of Levi (Mark 2:13–17, see above). This section treats the matter a little more directly, although the meaning of the passage is still debatable in terms of its logic. It is interesting that the whole incident described here essentially represents a trap. If Jesus affirms Roman taxation, he will offend his followers. If he rejects it, he will face charges of treason. Because the incident hinges on such particular circumstances, we should be cautious about applying the passage to dissimilar contemporary situations.

The response of Jesus to the trap revolves around the concepts of image and ownership. Examining the common denarius coin (essentially a day's wage), Jesus asks whose "image" (or even "icon") is upon the coin. The point of the question is probably to allude deliberately to Genesis 1:26–27 (humans made in the image of God) in order to create a contrast. Coins bear the image of the emperor, but humans bear the image of God. Give to the emperor what is his (money), but give to God what is his (our very lives). The core element, that humans bear the *imago Dei,* is unstated, but it is surely implied by the parallelism built into the logic of the argument.

In using such argumentation, Jesus subordinates the taxation issue to the greater demand of God upon our lives, but he does not thereby deny the validity of taxation, even that of the potentially abusive Roman system. Nor does he deny that money belongs to God. If money belongs to Caesar, it belongs even more to God because Caesar himself is under God's authority (Rom. 13:1–17; 1 Pet. 2:13–14). This passage is no warrant for the often expressed fallacy that business is business and religion is religion. As we have seen, God recognizes no sacred-secular divide. You cannot pretend to follow Christ by acting as if he cares nothing about your work. Jesus is not proclaiming license to do as you please at work, but peace about the things you cannot control. You can control whether you defraud others in your work (Mark 10:18), so don't do it. You cannot control whether you have to pay taxes (Mark 12:17), so pay them. In this passage, Jesus doesn't say what your obligation might be if you can control (or influence) your taxes, for example, if you are a Roman senator or a voter in a twenty-first-century democracy. (This incident is discussed in greater depth under "Luke 20:20–26" in "Luke and Work.")

The Cross and Resurrection (Mark 14:32–16:8)

The topics of status and grace return to the fore as Jesus faces his trial and crucifixion. "The Son of Man came not to be served but to serve, and to give his life a ransom for many" (Mark 10:45). Even for him the path of service requires renouncing all status:

> "The Son of Man will be handed over to the chief priests and the scribes, and they will condemn him to death; then they will hand him over to the Gentiles; they will mock him, and spit upon him, and flog him, and kill him; and after three days he will rise again." (Mark 10:33–34)

The people—correctly—proclaim Jesus as Messiah and King (Mark 11:8–11). But he sets aside this status and submits to false accusations by the Jewish council (Mark 14:53–65), an inept trial by the Roman government (Mark 15:1–15), and death at the hands of the humanity he came to save (Mark 15:21–41). His own disciples betray (Mark 14:43–49), deny (Mark 14:66–72), and desert him (Mark 14:50–51), except for a number of the women who had supported his work all along. He takes the absolute lowest place, forsaken by God and men and women, in order to grant us eternal life. At the bitter end, he feels abandoned by God himself (Mark 15:34). Mark, alone among the Gospels, records him crying the words of Psalm 22:1, "My God, my God, why have you forsaken me?" (Mark 15:34). On the cross, Jesus' final work is to absorb all of the world's forsakenness. Perhaps being misunderstood, mocked, and deserted was as hard on him as was being put to death. He was aware that his death would be overcome in a few days, yet the misunderstanding, mockery, and desertion continue to this day.

Many today also feel abandoned by friends, family, society, even God. The sense of abandonment at work can feel very strong. We can be marginalized by co-workers, crushed by labor and danger, anxious about our performance, frightened by the prospect of layoffs, and made desperate by inadequate pay and meager benefits, as was so memorably described in Studs Terkel's book, *Working*. The words of Sharon Atkins, a receptionist in Terkel's book, speak for many people: "I'd cry in the morning. I didn't want to get up. I'd dread Fridays because Monday was always looming over me. Another five days ahead of me. There never seemed to be any end to it. Why am I doing this?"[25]

But God's grace overcomes even the most crushing blows of work and life for those who will accept it. God's grace touches people from the immediate moment of Jesus' submission, when the centurion recognizes, "Truly this man was God's Son!" (Mark 15:39). Grace triumphs over death itself when Jesus is restored to life. The women receive word from God that "he has been raised" (Mark 16:6). In the section on Mark 1:1–13, we noted the abruptness of the ending. This is not a pretty story for religious pageants but God's gut-wrenching intervention in the grit and grime of our ragged lives and work. The busted tomb of the crucified criminal is more proof than most of us can stand that "many who are first will be last, and the last will be first" (Mark 10:31). Yet this amazing grace is the one way our work can yield "a hundredfold now in this age" and our lives lead into "the age to come, eternal life" (Mark 10:30). No wonder that "terror and amazement had seized them; and they said nothing to anyone, for they were afraid" (Mark 16:8).

Conclusion to Mark

The Gospel of Mark is not organized as an instruction manual for human work, but work is visible on every page. We have drawn out some of the most significant threads in this tapestry of life and labor, and applied them to issues of twenty-first-century work. There are many kinds of work, and many contexts in which people work. The unifying theme is that all of us are called to the work of growing, restoring, and governing God's creation, even while we await the final accomplishment of God's intent for the world when Christ returns.

---

[25] Studs Terkel, *Working* (New York: The New Press, 1972), 31.

Within this grand outline, it is striking that much of Mark's narrative revolves around identity themes. Mark shows that entering the kingdom of God requires transformation in our personal identity and communal relationships. Issues of status and identity were wrapped up with wealth and employment in the ancient world in a much more formal way than is the case today. But the underlying dynamics have not changed radically. Issues of status still influence our choices, decisions, and goals as workers. Roles, labels, affiliations, and relationships all factor into our employment and can cause us to make decisions for better or worse. We can all be vulnerable to the desire to assert our place in society by means of our property, wealth, or potential influence, and this, in turn, can affect our vocational decisions. All of these elements factor into our sense of identity, of who we are. Jesus' challenge to be ready to relinquish the claims of earthly status is, therefore, of fundamental significance. Relatively few may be called to the particular choices made by the twelve disciples, to leave their employment entirely, but the challenge to subordinate worldly identity to the demands of the kingdom is universal. Self-denial is the essence of following Jesus. Such an attitude involves the refusal to allow our identity to be determined by our status in a fallen world.

Such a radical self-denial is impossible without grace. God's grace is the miracle that transforms life and work, so that we are capable of living and serving in God's kingdom while we dwell in a fallen world. Yet God's grace seldom comes through instantaneous transformation. The narrative of the disciples is one of failure and restoration, of eventual, not immediate, change. Like them, our service in the kingdom of God remains marred by sin and failure. Like them, we find it necessary to repent of much along the way. Perhaps, though, we will also be like them in leaving a lasting legacy in the world, a kingdom whose borders have been expanded by our activity, and whose life has been enriched by our citizenship. As hard as it is to give up the things that inhibit us from following Christ to the full in our work, we find that serving him in our work is far more rewarding (Mark 10:29–32) than serving ourselves and our follies.

LUKE AND WORK

Introduction to Luke

The Gospel of Luke proclaims Jesus as the king who is coming into the world. Appointed by God, his rule will put right everything that has gone wrong following the rebellion and fall of humanity that began with Adam and Eve. At present, much of the world is governed by rebels against God's authority. Yet this world is God's kingdom nonetheless, and the stuff of daily life—including work—is the stuff of God's kingdom. God cares very deeply about the governance, productivity, justice, and culture of his world.

Jesus is both the king and model for all those who hold lesser authority. Although Christians are familiar with referring to Jesus as "king," somehow for many of us this title has come to seem primarily religious, rather than referring to an actual kingdom. We say that Jesus is the king, but we often mean that he is the king of the priests. We think of him as the founder of a religion, but Luke demonstrates that he is the re-founder of a realm—the kingdom of God on earth. When Jesus is personally present, even Satan and his minions acknowledge his rule (e.g., Luke 8:32) and his power is unchallengeable. After he returns, temporarily, to heaven, his model shows the citizens of his kingdom how to exercise authority and power in his stead.

Jesus' leadership extends to every aspect of life, including work. It is no surprise, then, that Luke's Gospel has wide application to work. Luke pays deep attention to work-related topics such as wealth and power, economics, government, conflict, leadership, productivity and provision, and investment, as we will discuss. We will proceed roughly in the order of Luke's text, occasionally taking passages out of order so we can consider them in a unit with other passages sharing the same theme. We will not attempt to discuss the passages that contribute little to an understanding of work, workers, and workplaces. It may prove surprising how much of Luke's Gospel turns out to be related to work.

The Kingdom of God Shows Up at Work (Luke 1–5)

God at Work (Luke 1–2; 4)

Zechariah's Surprising Day at Work (Luke 1:8–25)

Luke's Gospel begins in a workplace. This continues Yahweh's long history of appearing in workplaces (e.g., Gen. 2:19–20; Exod. 3:1–5). Zechariah is visited by the angel Gabriel on the most important workday of his life—the day he was chosen to minister in the holy place of the Jerusalem temple (Luke 1:8). While we may not be accustomed to thinking of the temple as a place of labor, the priests and Levites there were engaged in butchery (the sacrificial animals did not kill themselves), cooking, janitorial work, accounting, and a wide variety of other activities. The temple was not simply a religious center, but the center of Jewish economic and social life. Zechariah is impacted deeply by his encounter with the Lord—he is unable to speak until he has given witness to the truth of God's word.

The Good Shepherd Appears among the Shepherds (Luke 2:8–20)

The next workplace encounter takes place a few miles down the road from the temple. A group of shepherds watching their flocks by night are visited by an angelic host announcing the birth of Jesus (Luke 2:9). Shepherds were generally regarded as disreputable, and others looked down on them. But God looks down on them with favor. Like Zechariah the priest, the shepherds have their workday interrupted by God in a surprising way. Luke describes a reality in which an encounter with the Lord is not reserved for Sundays, retreats, or mission trips. Instead, each moment appears as a moment of potential in which God can reveal himself. The daily grind may serve to dull our spiritual senses, like the people of Lot's generation whose routines of "eating and drinking, buying and selling, planting and building" blinded them to the coming judgment on their city (Luke 17:28–30).[1] But God is able to break into the midst of everyday life with his goodness and glory.

---

[1] Note also the men in the parable who refuse the invitation to the wedding banquet because they need to look at their recently purchased field (Luke 14:18) and oxen (Luke 14:19). Rather than being open to find God in their work, they use work as a means to avoid God.

Jesus' Job Description: King (Luke 1:26–56; 4:14–22)

If it seems strange for God to announce his plan to save the world in the midst of two workplaces, it might seem even stranger that he introduces Jesus with a job description. But he does, when the angel Gabriel tells Mary she is to give birth to a son: "He will be great, and will be called the Son of the Most High and the Lord God will give to him the throne of his ancestor David. He will reign over the house of Jacob forever, and of his kingdom there will be no end" (Luke 1:32–33).

While we may be unaccustomed to thinking of "king of Israel" as Jesus' job, it is definitely his work according to Luke's Gospel. Details of his work as king are given: performing mighty deeds, scattering the proud, bringing down rulers from their thrones, lifting up the humble, filling the empty with good things, sending the rich away empty, helping Israel, and showing mercy to Abraham's descendants (Luke 1:51–55). These famous verses, often called the Magnificat, portray Jesus as a king exercising economic, political, and perhaps even military power. Unlike the corrupt kings of the fallen world, he employs his power to benefit his most vulnerable subjects. He does not curry favor with the powerful and well-connected in order to shore up his dynasty. He does not oppress his people or tax them to support luxurious habits. He establishes a properly governed realm where the land yields good things for all people, safety for God's people, and mercy to those who repent of evil. He is the king that Israel never had.

Later, Jesus confirms this job description when he applies Isaiah 61:1–2 to himself: "The Spirit of the Lord is upon me, because he has anointed me to bring good news to the poor. He has sent me to proclaim release to the captives and recovery of sight to the blind, to let the oppressed go free, to proclaim the year of the Lord's favor" (Luke 4:18–19). These are political and governmental tasks. Thus, in Luke at least, Jesus' occupation is more closely related to present-day political work than it is to today's pastoral or religious professions.[2] Jesus is

---

[2] Even those books that call Christ the "head of the church"—that is, Ephesians (4:15, 5:23) and Colossians (1:18)—also speak of him as the "head over everything" (Eph. 1:22, NIV) and the "head over every ruler and authority" (Col. 2:10). Christ is the chief of state, the head of all things—or will be, when the redemption of the world is complete—of which the church is a special subset.

highly respectful of the priests and their special role in God's order, but he does not primarily identify himself as one of them (Luke 5:14; 17:14).

The tasks Jesus claims for himself benefit people in need. Unlike the rulers of the fallen world, he rules on behalf of the poor, the prisoners, the blind, the oppressed, and those who have fallen into debt (whose lands are returned to them during the year of the Lord's favor; see Lev. 25:8–13). His concern is not only for people in desperate need. He cares for people in every station and condition, as we will see. But his concern for the poor, the suffering, and the powerless distinguishes him starkly from the rulers he has come to displace.

Jesus Calls People at Work (Luke 5:1–11, 27–32)

Twice Jesus goes to people's workplaces to call them to follow him. The first is when Jesus gets some fishermen to interrupt their work and let him use their boat as a podium. Then he gives them some excellent fishing tips and suddenly calls them to become his first disciples (Luke 5:1–11). The second is when he calls Levi, who is at his work of collecting taxes (Luke 5:27–32). These people are called to follow Jesus by leaving their professions. We tend to think of them as full-time church workers, but full-time "ambassadors" (2 Cor. 5:20) would be a more accurate description. Although these individuals are called to a particular kind of work in Jesus' kingdom, Luke isn't saying that some callings (e.g., preaching) are higher than others (e.g., fishing). Some of Jesus' followers—like Peter, John, and Levi—follow Jesus by leaving their current employment (Luke 5:11). We will soon meet others—such as Mary and Martha (Luke 10:38–41), another tax collector named Zacchaeus (Luke 19:1–10), and a Roman military officer (Luke 1–10)—who follow Jesus by living transformed lives in their present occupations. In one case (Luke 8:26–39), Jesus commands a person *not* to leave his home and travel around with him.

Those who travel with Jesus apparently cease wage-earning work and depend on donations for provision (Luke 9:1–6; 10:1–24). But this is not a sign that the highest form of discipleship is to leave our jobs. It is a specific call to these individuals and a reminder that all our provision is from God, even if he typically provides for us through conventional employment. There are many models for following Christ in our various occupations. (For more about Jesus' calling of the disciples, see "Mark 1:16–20" in "Mark and Work" and "Matthew 3–4" in "Matthew and Work.")

Besides appearing in workplaces, Jesus also sets many of his parables in workplaces, including the parables of the new patches/wineskins (Luke 5:36–39), the wise and foolish builders (Luke 6:46–49), the sower (Luke 8:4–15), the watchful servants (Luke 12:35–41), the wicked servant (Luke 12:42–47), the mustard seed (Luke 13:18–19), the yeast (Luke 13:20–21), the lost sheep (Luke 15:1–7), the lost coin (Luke 15:8–10), the prodigal son (Luke 15:11–32), and the wicked tenants (Luke 20:9–19). Workplaces are where Jesus turns when he wants to say, "The kingdom of God is like . . ." These passages are not generally meant to teach about the workplaces in which they are set, although sometimes they do provide a bit of workplace guidance. Rather, Jesus uses familiar aspects of workplaces primarily to make points about God's kingdom that transcend the parables' particular settings. This suggests that ordinary work has great significance and value in Jesus' eyes. Otherwise it would make no sense to illustrate God's kingdom in workplace terms.

John the Baptist Teaches Workplace Ethics (Luke 3:8–14)

Much of Luke consists of Jesus' teaching. As it happens, the first teaching in Luke is directly about work, although it comes from John the Baptist rather than Jesus. John exhorts his audience to "bear fruits worthy of repentance" (Luke 3:8) lest they face judgment. When they ask specifically, "What should we do?" (Luke 3:10, 12, 14), John gives economic, not religious, responses. First, he tells those who have an abundance of possessions (two tunics or ample food) to share with those who have nothing (Luke 3:10). He then gives instructions to tax collectors and soldiers, relating directly to their work. Tax collectors should collect only what they are required to, rather than padding the tax bill and pocketing the difference. Soldiers should not use their power to extort money and accuse people falsely. They should be content with their pay (Luke 3:13–14).

When John tells the tax collectors, "Collect no more than the amount prescribed for you" (Luke 3:13), he was speaking radical words to a profession marked by entrenched, systemic injustice. Taxes throughout Palestine were gathered through a system of "tax farming" in which governors and other high-level officials outsourced the right to collect taxes in their jurisdictions.[3] In order to win a contract, a prospective tax collector would have to agree to give the official a certain amount over and above the actual Roman tax. Likewise, the tax collectors' own profits were the amounts they charged over and above what they passed up to the governmental officials. Since the people had no way to know what the actual Roman tax was, they had to pay whatever the tax collector assessed them. It would have been hard to resist the temptation for self-enrichment, and almost impossible to win bids without offering fat profits to the governmental officials.

Notice that John does not offer them the option to stop being tax collectors. The situation is similar for those Luke calls "soldiers." These are probably not disciplined Roman soldiers but employees of Herod, who at that time ruled Galilee as a client king for Rome. Herod's soldiers could (and did) use their authority to intimidate, extort, and secure self-gain. John's instruction to these workers is to bring justice to a system deeply marked by injustice. We should not underestimate how difficult that would have been. Holding citizenship in God's kingdom while living under the rule of kings of the fallen world can be dangerous and difficult.

Jesus Is Tempted to Abandon Serving God (Luke 4:1–13)

Just before Jesus begins his work as king, Satan tempts him to abandon his allegiance to God. Jesus goes to the wilderness, where he fasts for forty days (Luke 4:2). Then he faces the same temptations the people of

---

[3] John Nolland, *Luke 1–9:20*, vol. 35a, *Word Biblical Commentary* (Nashville: Thomas Nelson, 1989), 150: "Tax collectors had to work in a social context whose very structures were defined by graft and corruption. The honest tax collector would face problems akin to those faced today by a businessman seeking to operate without graft in relation to the bureaucracies of certain countries." Robert H. Stein, *Luke* (Nashville: Broadman, 1992), 134: "The soldiers probably were not Romans but Jews whom Herod Antipas employed (cf. Josephus, *Antiquities* 18.5.1 [18.113]) perhaps to assist tax collectors in their duties. Soldiers were . . . not required to resign [by Jesus] but to avoid the sins of their professions, i.e., violent intimidation ('extort'), robbing by false accusation, and dissatisfaction with wages (or perhaps 'rations')."

Israel faced in the wilderness of Sinai. (The answers Jesus gives to Satan are all quotes from Deuteronomy 6–8, which tells the story of Israel in the wilderness.) First, he is tempted to trust in his own power to satisfy his needs, rather than trusting in God's provision (Luke 4:1–3; Deut. 8:3, 17–20): "If you are the Son of God, command this stone to become a loaf of bread" (Luke 4:3). Second, he is tempted to switch his allegiance to someone (Satan) who flatters him with shortcuts to power and glory (Luke 4:5–8; Deut. 6:13; 7:1–26): "If you, then, will worship me, it will all be yours." Third, he is tempted to question whether God really is with him, and therefore to try forcing God's hand in desperation (Luke 4:9–12; Deut. 6:16–25): "If you are the Son of God, throw yourself down from here" (the temple). Unlike Israel, Jesus resists these temptations by relying on God's word. He is the man that the people of Israel—like Adam and Eve before them—were meant to be, but never were.

As parallels to the temptations of Israel in Deuteronomy 6–8, these temptations are not unique to Jesus. He experiences them much as we all do. "For we do not have a high priest who is unable to sympathize with our weaknesses, but we have one who in every respect has been tested as we are, yet without sin" (Heb. 4:15). Like Israel, and like Jesus, we can expect to be tempted as well, in work as in all of life.

The temptation to work solely to meet our own needs is very high at work. Work *is* intended to meet our needs (2 Thess. 3:10), but not *only* to meet our needs. Our work is meant to serve others also. Unlike Jesus, we do not have the option of self-service by means of miracles. But we can be tempted to work just enough for the paycheck, to quit when things get difficult, to shirk our share of the load, or to ignore the burden our poor work habits force others to carry. The temptation to take shortcuts is also high at work.

The temptation to question God's presence and power in our work may be the greatest of these temptations. Jesus was tempted to test God by forcing his hand. We do the same thing when we become lazy or foolish and expect God to take care of us. Occasionally this happens when someone decides God has called him or her to some profession or position, and then sits around waiting for God to make it happen. But we are probably more likely to be tempted by giving up on God's presence and power in our work. We may think our work means nothing to God, or that God only cares about our church life, or that we cannot pray for God's help for the day-to-day activities of work. Jesus expected God to participate in his work every day, but he did not demand that God do the work for him.

The entire episode begins with God's Spirit leading Jesus into the wilderness to fast for forty days. Then, as now, fasting and going on a retreat was a way to draw close to God before embarking on a major life change. Jesus was about to begin his work as king, and he wanted to receive God's power, wisdom, and presence before he started. This was successful. When Satan tempted Jesus, he had spent forty days in God's spirit. He was fully prepared to resist. Yet his fast also made the temptation more visceral: "He was famished" (Luke 4:2). Temptation often comes upon us far sooner than we expect, even at the beginning of our working lives. We may be tempted to enroll in a get-rich-quick scheme, instead of starting at the bottom of the ladder in a genuinely productive profession. We may come to face to face with our own weaknesses for the first time, and be tempted to compensate by cheating or bullying or deception. We may think we can't get the job we want with the skills we have, so we are tempted to misrepresent ourselves or fabricate qualifications. We may take a lucrative but unfulfilling position "just for a few years, until I'm settled," in the fantasy that we will later do something more in line with our calling.

Preparation is the key to victory over temptation. Temptations usually come without warning. You may be ordered to submit a false report. You may be offered confidential information today that will be public knowledge tomorrow. An unlocked door may offer a sudden opportunity to take something that isn't yours. The pressure to join in gossiping about a co-worker may arise suddenly during lunch break. The best preparation is to imagine possible scenarios in advance and, in prayer, plan how to respond to them, perhaps even write them down along with the responses you commit to God. Another protection is to have a group of people who know you intimately, whom you can call on short notice to discuss your temptation. If you can let them know before you act, they may help you through the temptation. Jesus, being in communion with his Father in the power of the Holy Spirit, faced his temptations with the support of his peer community—if we may so describe the Trinity.

Our temptations are not identical to Jesus', even if they have broad similarities. We all have our own temptations, large and small, depending on who we are, our circumstances, and the nature of our work. None is us is the Son of God, yet how we respond to temptation has life-changing consequences. Imagine the consequences if Jesus had turned aside from his calling as God's king and had spent his life creating luxuries for himself, or doing the bidding of the master of evil, or lying around waiting for the Father to do his work for him.

Healing in Luke

In Jesus' day, as now, the work of healing and health was essential. Jesus heals people in thirteen episodes in the Gospel of Luke: 4:31–37; 4:38–44; 5:12–16; 5:17–26; 7:1–10; 7:11–17; 7:21; 8:26–39; 8:40–56; 9:37–45; 13:10–17; 17:11–19; and 18:35–43. By doing so, he brings wellness to suffering people, as he announced he would do when he took on the mantle of king. In addition, the healings are actualizations of the coming kingdom of God, in which there will be no sickness (Rev. 21:4). God not only *commands* people to work for others' benefit, he *empowers* people to do so. God's power is not restricted to Jesus himself, for in two passages Jesus empowers his followers to heal people (Luke 9:1–6, 10:9). Yet all the healings depend on God's power. Theologian Jürgen Moltmann sums this up beautifully: "Jesus' healings are not supernatural miracles in a natural world. They are the only truly 'natural' thing in a world that is unnatural, demonized, and wounded."[4] They are a tangible sign that God is putting the world back to right.

The healings reported in the Gospels are generally miraculous. But Christians' nonmiraculous efforts to restore human bodies can also be seen as extensions of Jesus' life-giving ministry. It would be a mistake not to notice how important healing is to the redemptive work of God's kingdom. This work is performed daily by doctors, nurses, technologists, claims processors, hospital parking lot attendants, and countless others whose work makes healing possible. Luke himself was a physician

---

[4] Jürgen Moltmann, *The Way of Jesus Christ* (Minneapolis: Fortress Press, 1995), 69.

(Col. 4:14), and we can imagine his particular interest in healing. However, it would be a mistake to infer that the healing professions are inherently higher callings than other professions.

Sabbath and Work (Luke 6:1–11; 13:10–17)

The Sabbath is an essential part of the biblical understanding of work, and Jesus teaches about the Sabbath in the Gospel of Luke. Work and rest are not opposing forces, but elements of a rhythm that make good work and true recreation possible. Ideally, that rhythm meets people's needs for provision and health, but in a fallen world, there are times when it does not.

Lord of the Sabbath (Luke 6:1–11)

In Luke 6:1–5, it is the Sabbath, and Jesus and his disciples are hungry. They pluck heads of grain in a field, rub them in their hands, and eat the kernels. Some Pharisees complain that this constitutes threshing and is therefore working on the Sabbath. Jesus responds that David and his companions also broke the sacred rules when they were hungry, entering the house of God and eating the consecrated bread that only priests were allowed to eat. We might imagine that the connection between these two episodes is hunger. When you are hungry it is permissible to work to feed yourself, even if it means working on the Sabbath. But Jesus draws a somewhat different conclusion: "The Son of Man is Lord of the sabbath" (Luke 6:5). This suggests that keeping the Sabbath is grounded in understanding God's heart, rather than developing increasingly detailed rules and exceptions.

Set Free on the Sabbath (Luke 13:10–17)

Other healings Jesus performs on the Sabbath are described in Luke 6:9 and 14:5. Nonetheless, it would be hard to piece together a theology of the Sabbath from only the events in Luke. But we can observe that Jesus anchors his understanding of the Sabbath in the needs of people. Human needs come before keeping the Sabbath, even though keeping the Sabbath is one of the Ten Commandments. Yet by meeting human needs on the Sabbath, the commandment is fulfilled, not abolished. The healing of the crippled woman on the Sabbath provides a particularly rich example of this. "There are six days on which work ought to be done," the indignant synagogue ruler chides the crowd. "Come on those days and be cured, and not on the sabbath day" (Luke 13:14). Jesus' reply begins with the law. If people water their animals on the Sabbath, as was lawful, "ought not this woman, a daughter of Abraham whom Satan bound for eighteen long years, be set free from this bondage on the sabbath day?" (Luke 13:16). (Additional discussions of the Sabbath—in some cases with a differing perspective—can be found under "Mark 1:21–45" and "Mark 2:23–3:6" in "Mark and Work.")

The Ethics of Conflict (Luke 6:27–36; 17:3–4)

Do Good to Those Who Hate You (Luke 6:27–36)

All workplaces experience conflict. In Luke 6:27–36, Jesus addresses situations of conflict. "Love your enemies, do good to those who hate you, bless those who curse you, pray for those who abuse you" (Luke 6:27–28). Luke leaves no doubt that this is a teaching for the economic world, for he specifically relates it to lending money: "Lend [to your enemies], expecting nothing in return" (Luke 6:35). This doesn't seem like a viable commercial lending strategy, but perhaps we can understand it at a more abstract level. Christians must not use their power to crush people with whom they are in conflict. Instead, they must actively work for their good. This can apply to the workplace at two levels.

At the individual level, it means that we must work for the good of those with whom we are in conflict. This does not mean avoiding conflict or withdrawing from competition. But it does mean, for example, that if you are competing with a co-worker for promotion, you must help your co-worker/opponent do their work as well as they can, while trying to do yours even better.

At the corporate level, it means not crushing your competition, suppliers, or customers, especially with unfair or unproductive actions such as frivolous lawsuits, monopolization, false rumors, stock manipulation, and the like. Every occupation has its own circumstances, and it would be foolish to draw a one-size-fits-all application from this passage in Luke. Competing hard in business via intentional fraud might be different from competing hard in basketball via an intentional foul. Therefore, an essential element of believers' participation in an occupation is to try to work out what the proper modes of conflict and competition are in light of Jesus' teaching.

Rebuke, Repent, Forgive (Luke 17:3–4)

Later, Jesus again addresses interpersonal conflict: "If your brother or sister sins against you, rebuke them; and if they repent, forgive them" (Luke 17:3, NIV). We shouldn't take this as family therapy only, because Jesus applies the term "brother" to all those who follow him (Mark 3:35). It is good organizational behavior to confront people directly and to restore good relationships when the conflict is resolved. But the next verse breaks the bounds of common sense. "If the same person sins against you seven times a day, and turns back to you seven times and says, 'I repent,' you must forgive" (Luke 17:4). In fact, Jesus not only commands forgiveness, but the absence of judgment in the first place. "Do not judge, and you will not be judged; do not condemn, and you will not be condemned" (Luke 6:37). "Why do you see the speck of sawdust in your neighbor's eye, but do not notice the log in your own eye?" (Luke 6:41).

Would it be wise to be so nonjudgmental at work? Isn't sound judgment a requirement for good organizational governance and performance? Perhaps Jesus is talking about giving up not good judgment but judgmentalism and condemnation—the hypocritical attitude that the problems around us are entirely someone else's fault. Perhaps Jesus doesn't so much mean, "Ignore repeated moral lapses or incompetence," so much as, "Ask yourself how your actions may have contributed to the problem." Perhaps he doesn't mean, "Don't assess others' performance," so much as, "Figure out what you can do to help those around you succeed." Perhaps Jesus' point is not leniency but mercy: "Do to others as you would have them do to you" (Luke 6:31).

God's Provision (Luke 9:10–17; 12:4–7, 22–31)

Throughout Luke, Jesus teaches that living in God's kingdom means looking to God, rather than human effort, as the ultimate source of the things we need for life. Our labor is not optional, but neither is it absolute. Our labor is always a participation in the grace of God's provision.

Jesus Feeds Five Thousand (Luke 9:10–17)

Jesus demonstrates this in actions before he teaches it in words. In the feeding of the five thousand (Luke 9:10–17), God, in the person of Jesus, takes responsibility for meeting the crowd's need for food. He does it because they are hungry. Exactly how Jesus works this miracle is not stated. He makes use of ordinary food—the five loaves of bread and two fish—and by God's power, a little bit of food becomes enough to feed so many people. Some of Jesus' disciples (the fishermen) were in the food service profession and others (e.g., Levi the tax collector) were in civil service. He employs their accustomed labor, as they organize the crowd and serve the bread and fish. Jesus incorporates, rather than replaces, the ordinary human means of providing food, and the results are miraculously successful. Human work is capable of doing good or doing harm. When we do as Jesus directs, our work is good. As we so often see in the Gospel of Luke, God brings miraculous results out of ordinary work—in this case, the work of providing the necessities of life.

Jesus Teaches about God's Provision (Luke 12:4–7, 22–31)

Later, Jesus teaches about God's provision: "I tell you, do not worry about your life, what you will eat, or about your body, what you will wear. . . . Can any of you by worrying add a single hour to your span of life? If then you are not able to do so small a thing as that, why do you worry about the rest?" (Luke 12:22, 25–26). Jesus offers this as plain common sense. Since worrying cannot add so much as an hour to your life, why worry? Jesus doesn't say not to work, only not to worry about whether your work will provide enough to meet your needs.

In an economy of plenty, this is excellent advice. Many of us are driven by worry to labor in jobs we don't like, keeping hours that detract from our enjoyment of life, neglecting the needs of others around us. To us, the goal doesn't seem like "more" money but rather "enough" money, enough to feel secure. Yet seldom do we actually feel secure, no matter how much more money we make. In fact, it's often true that the more successful we are at bringing in more money, the less secure we feel because we now have more to lose. It's almost as if we would be better off if we had something genuine to worry about, as do the poor ("Blessed are you who are hungry now, for you will be filled," Luke 6:21). To break out of this rut, Jesus says to "strive for [God's] kingdom, and these things will be given to you as well" (Luke 12:31). Why? Because if your ultimate goal is God's kingdom, then you have the assurance that your ultimate goal will be met. And feeling that assurance, you can recognize that the money you make actually is enough, that God is providing for your needs. To earn a million dollars and be afraid you may lose it is like being a million dollars in debt. To earn a thousand dollars and to know that you will ultimately be fine is like getting a thousand-dollar gift.

But what if you don't have a thousand dollars? About a third of the world's population subsists on less than a thousand dollars a year.[5] These people may have enough to live on today, but face the threat of hunger or worse at any moment, whether or not they are believers. It is difficult to reconcile the hard fact of poverty and starvation with God's promise of provision. Jesus is not ignorant of this situation. "Sell your possessions and give to the poor," he says (Luke 12:33, NIV), for he knows that some people are desperately poor. That's why we must give to them. Perhaps if all Jesus' followers used our work and wealth to alleviate and prevent poverty, we would become the means of God's provision for the desperately poor. But since Christians have not done so, we will not pretend to speak here on behalf of people who are so poor that their provision is doubtful. Instead, let us ask whether our own provision is presently in doubt. Is our worry in proportion to any genuine danger of lacking what we really need? Are the things we worry about genuine needs? Are the things we worry about for ourselves remotely comparable to the things the desperately poor need that we do nothing to provide for them? If not, then anything but Jesus' advice not to worry about the necessities of life would be foolhardy.

---

[5] Peter Greer and Phil Smith, *The Poor Will Be Glad* (Grand Rapids: Zondervan, 2009), 29.

The Shrewd Manager and the Prodigal Son (Luke 16:1–13; 15:11–32)

The Parable of the Shrewd Manager (Luke 16:1–13)

The key to security about the things we need is not anxious earning and saving, but trustworthy service and spending. If God can trust us to spend our money to meet the needs of others, then the money we our-selves need will also be provided. This is the point of the parable of the dishonest manager. In it, a manager squanders his master's property and, as a result, is notified he will be fired. He uses his last days on the job to defraud his master further, but there is a strange twist to how he does it. He does not try to steal from his master. Perhaps he knows it will be im-possible to take anything with him when he leaves the estate. Instead, he fraudulently reduces the debts of his masters' debtors, hoping that they will reciprocate the favor and provide for him when he is unemployed.

Like the dishonest manager, we cannot take anything with us when we depart this life. Even during this life our savings can be destroyed by hyperinflation, market crashes, theft, confiscation, lawsuits, war, and natural disaster. Therefore, building up large savings offers no real se-curity. Instead, we should spend our wealth to provide for other people, and depend on them to do the same for us when the need arises. "Make friends for yourselves by means of dishonest wealth so that when it is gone, they may welcome you into the eternal homes" (Luke 16:9). By pro-viding for his master's debtors, the dishonest steward is creating friend-ships. Mutual fraud is probably not the best way to build relationships. But apparently it is better than not building relationships at all. Build-ing relationships is far more effective for gaining security than building wealth is. The word *eternal* signifies that good relationships help us in times of trouble in this life, and they will also endure into eternal life.

An extreme example of this principle occurs whenever war, terror, or disaster destroys the economic fabric of society. In a refugee camp, a prison, or a hyperinflated economy, the wealth you formerly may have had cannot procure even a crust of bread. But if you have provided for others, you may find them providing for you in your most difficult hour. Note that the people the dishonest manager helps are not wealthy people.

They are debtors. The dishonest manager is not depending on their riches but on the relationship of mutual dependence he has built with them.

Yet Jesus is *not* saying to depend on the fickle sentiments of people you may have helped over the years. The story turns quickly from the debtors to the master in the story (Luke 16:8), and Jesus endorses the master's maxim, "Whoever is faithful in a very little is faithful also in much" (Luke 16:10). This points to God as the guarantor that using money for relationships will lead to lasting security. When you build good relationships with other people, you come to have a good relationship with God. Jesus does not say which matters more to God, the generosity to the poor or the good relationships with people. Perhaps it is both: "If then you have not been faithful with the dishonest wealth, who will entrust to you the true riches?" (Luke 16:11). True riches are good relationships with people founded on our mutual adoption as God's children, and a good relationship with God is realized in generosity to the poor. Good relationships produce good fruit, which gives us greater ability to build good relationships and be generous to others. If God can trust you to be generous with a little bit of money and use it to build good relationships, he will be able to entrust you with greater resources.

This suggests that if you do not have enough savings to feel secure, the answer is not trying to save more. Instead, spend the little you have on generosity or hospitality. Other people's responses to your generosity and hospitality may bring you more security than saving more money would. Needless to say, this should be done wisely, in ways that truly benefit others, and not merely to assuage your conscience or flatter people targeted as future benefactors. In any case, your ultimate security is in God's generosity and hospitality.

Echoes of the Prodigal Son (Luke 15:11–32)

This may be surprising financial advice: Don't save, but spend what you have to draw closer to other people. Notice, however, that it comes immediately after the story of the prodigal son (Luke 15:11–32). In that story, the younger son wastes his entire fortune, while the older son saves his money so frugally that he can't even entertain his closest friends (Luke 15:29). The younger son's profligacy leads to ruin. Yet his squandering of the wealth leads him to turn to his father in utter dependence. The father's joy at having him back washes away any negative feelings he has about the son costing him half a fortune. By contrast, the older son's firm grasp on what's left of the family's wealth turns him away from a close relationship with his father.

In the stories of both the dishonest manager and the prodigal son, Jesus does not say that wealth is inherently bad. Rather, he says that the proper use of wealth is to spend it, preferably on God's purposes—but if not that, then on things that will increase our dependence on God.

Wealth in Luke

The last two passages move from the topic of provision to the topic of wealth. Although Jesus has nothing against wealth, he views wealth with suspicion. Market economies are predicated upon the generation, exchange, and accumulation of privately owned wealth. This reality is so deeply embedded in many societies that the pursuit and accumulation of personal wealth has become, for many, an end in itself. But, as we have seen, Jesus does not see the accumulation of wealth as a proper end in itself. Just as one's work (modeled upon the life of Jesus) must exhibit a profound concern for others and an unwillingness to use work-related power or authority only for self-gain, so also wealth must be used with a deep concern for neighbors. While Luke's second volume, Acts (see "Acts and Work"), has more wealth-related material, his Gospel also poses significant challenges to dominant assumptions about wealth.

Concern for the Wealthy (Luke 6:25; 12:13–21; 18:18–30)

Jesus' first problem with wealth is that it tends to displace God in the lives of wealthy people. "For where your treasure is, there your heart will be also" (Luke 12:34). Jesus wants people to recognize that their lives are defined not by what they have, but by God's love for them and his call upon their lives. Luke expects us—and the work we do—to be fundamentally transformed by our encounters with Jesus.

But having wealth seems to make us stubbornly resistant to any transformation of life. It affords us the means to maintain the status quo, to become independent, to do things our own way. True, or eternal, life is a life of relationship with God (and other people), and wealth that displaces God leads ultimately to eternal death. As Jesus said, "What does it profit them if they gain the whole world, but lose or forfeit themselves?" (Luke 9:25). The wealthy may be lured away from life with God by their own wealth, a fate that the poor escape. "Blessed are you who are poor, for yours is the kingdom of God," says Jesus (Luke 6:20). This is not a promise of future reward, but a statement of present reality. The poor have no wealth to stand in the way of loving God. But "woe to you who are full now, for you will be hungry" (Luke 6:25). "Be hungry" seems a bit of an understatement for "miss eternal life by putting God outside your sphere of interest," but that is clearly the implication. Yet perhaps there is hope even for the wretchedly rich.

The Parable of the Rich Fool (Luke 12:13–21)

The parable of the rich fool (Luke 12:13–21) takes up this theme dramatically. "The land of a rich man produced abundantly," too much to fit in the man's barns. "What should I do?" he worries, and he decides to tear down his barns and build bigger ones. He is among those who believe that having more wealth will lead to less worry about money. But before he discovers how empty his worrisome wealth is, he meets an even starker fate—death. As he prepares to die, God's mocking question is a double-edged sword, "The things you have prepared, whose will they be?" (Luke 12:20). One edge is the answer, "not yours," for the wealth he counted upon to satisfy him for many years will pass instantly to someone else. The other edge cuts even deeper, and it is the answer, "yours." You—the rich fool—will indeed get what you have prepared for yourself, a life after death without God, true death indeed. His wealth has prevented him from the need to develop a relationship with God, exhibited by his failure to even think of using his bumper crop to provide for those in need. "So it is with those who store up treasures for themselves but are not rich toward God" (Luke 12:21).

Friendship with God is seen here in economic terms. God's friends who are rich provide for God's friends who are poor. The rich fool's problem is that he hoards things *for himself, not producing jobs or prosperity for others.* This means both that he loves wealth instead of God, and that he is not generous toward the poor. We can imagine a rich person who truly loves God and holds wealth lightly, one who gives liberally to the needy, or better yet, invests money in producing genuine goods and services, employs a growing workforce, and treats people with justice and fairness in their work. In fact, we can find many such people in the Bible (for example, Joseph of Arimathea, Luke 23:50) and in the world around us. Such people are blessed both in life and afterwards. Yet we do not want to remove the sting of the parable: if it is possible to grow (economically and otherwise) with grace, it is also possible to grow only with greed; the final accounting is with God.

The Rich Ruler (Luke 18:18–30)

Jesus' encounter with the rich ruler (Luke 18:18–30) points to the possibility of redemption from the grip of wealth. This man has not let his riches entirely displace his desire for God. He begins by asking Jesus, "Good Teacher, what must I do to inherit eternal life?" In response, Jesus summarizes the Ten Commandments. "I have kept all these since my youth," replies the ruler (Luke 18:21), and Jesus accepts him at his word. Yet even so, Jesus sees the corrupting influence that wealth is working on the man. So he offers him a way to end wealth's pernicious influence. "Sell all that you own and distribute the money to the poor, and you will have treasure in heaven; then come, follow me" (Luke 18:22). Anyone whose deepest desire is for God would surely leap at the invitation to daily, personal intimacy with God's Son. But it is too late for the rich ruler—his love of wealth already exceeds his love for God. "He became sad; for he was very rich" (Luke 18:23). Jesus recognizes the symptoms and says, "How hard it is for those who have wealth to enter the kingdom of God! Indeed, it is easier for a camel to go through the eye of a needle than for someone who is rich to enter the kingdom of God" (Luke 18:24–25).

By contrast, the poor often show amazing generosity. The poor widow is able to give away everything she has for the love of God (Luke 21:1–4). This is no summary judgment by God against wealthy people, but an observation of the heavy grip of wealth's seductive power. The people standing near Jesus and the ruler also recognize the problem and despair over whether anyone can resist the lure of wealth, though they themselves have given away everything to follow Jesus (Luke 18:28). Jesus, however, does not despair, for "what is impossible for mortals is possible for God" (Luke 18:27). God himself is the source of strength for our desire to love God more than wealth.

Perhaps wealth's most insidious effect is that it can prevent us from desiring a better future. If you are wealthy, things are good as they are now. Change becomes a threat rather than an opportunity. In the case of the rich ruler, this blinds him to the possibility that life with Jesus could be incomparably wonderful. Jesus offers the rich ruler a new sense of identity and security. If he could only have imagined how that would more than make up for the loss of his wealth, perhaps he could have accepted Jesus' invitation. The punch line comes when the disciples speak of all they've given up, and Jesus promises them the overflowing riches of belonging to the kingdom of God. Even in this age, Jesus says, they will receive "very much more" in both resources and relationships, and in the coming age, eternal life (Luke 18:29–30). This is what the rich ruler is tragically missing out on. He can see only what he will lose, not what he will gain. (The story of the rich ruler is further discussed under "Mark 10:17–31" in "Mark and Work.")

Concern for the Poor (Luke 6:17–26; 16:19–31)

The well-being of the rich is not Jesus' only concern with regard to wealth. He also cares about the well-being of the poor. "Sell your possessions," he says, "and give alms [to the poor]. Make purses for yourselves that do not wear out, an unfailing treasure in heaven, where no thief comes near and no moth destroys" (Luke 12:33). If the hoarding of wealth is harming the rich, how much more is it harming the poor?

God's persistent concern for the poor and powerless is inherent in the Magnificat (Luke 1:46–56), the Sermon on the Plain (Luke 6:17–26), and indeed throughout Luke's Gospel. But Jesus brings it to a point in the parable of Lazarus and the rich man (Luke 16:19–31). This rich man dresses in grand clothes and lives in luxury, while he does nothing to help relieve Lazarus, who is dying of hunger and disease. Lazarus dies, but so, of course, does the rich man, which reminds us that wealth has no great power after all. The angels carry Lazarus to heaven, apparently for no reason other than his poverty (Luke 16:22), unless perhaps for a love of God that was never displaced by wealth. The rich man goes to Hades, apparently for no reason other than his wealth (Luke 16:23), unless perhaps for a love of wealth that drove out any room for God or other people. The implication is strong that the rich man's duty was to care for Lazarus' needs when he was able (Luke 16:25). Perhaps by so doing, he could have found room again in himself for a right relationship with God and avoided his miserable end. Further, like many of the rich, he cared for his family, wanting to warn them of the judgment to come, but his care for God's wider family as revealed in the law and prophets was sadly lacking, and not even one returning from the dead could remedy that.

Generosity: The Secret to Breaking Wealth's Grip (Luke 10:38–42; 14:12–14; 24:13–35)

This suggests that God's secret weapon is generosity. If by God's power you can be generous, wealth begins to lose its grip on you. We have already seen how deeply generosity worked in the heart of the poor widow. It is much harder for the rich to be generous, but Jesus teaches how generosity might be possible for them too. One crucial path to generosity is to give to people who are too poor to pay you back.

> [Jesus] said also to the one who had invited him, "When you give a luncheon or dinner, do not invite your friends or your brothers or relatives or your rich neighbors, in case they may invite you in return, and you would be repaid. But when you give a banquet, invite the poor, the crippled, the lame, and the blind. And you will be blessed, because they cannot repay you, for you will be repaid at the resurrection of the righteous." (Luke 14:12–14)

Generosity that earns favors in return is not generosity but favor-buying. Real generosity is giving when no payback is possible, and this is what is rewarded in eternity. Of course, the reward in heaven could be taken as a kind of delayed gratification rather than true generosity: you give because you expect to be paid back at the resurrection, rather than during earthly life. This seems like a wiser sort of favor-buying, but favor-buying nonetheless. Jesus' words do not rule out interpreting generosity as

eternal favor-buying, but there is a deeper, more satisfying interpretation. True generosity—the kind that doesn't expect to be paid back in
this life or the next—breaks wealth's God-displacing grip. When you
give away money, money releases its grip on you, but only if you put the
money permanently beyond your reach. This is a psychological reality,
as well as a material and spiritual one. Generosity allows room for God
to be your God again, and this leads to the true reward of the resurrection—eternal life with God.

Mary and Martha (Luke 10:38–42)

The story of Martha and Mary (Luke 10:38–42) also puts generosity
in the context of love for God. Martha works to prepare dinner, while
Mary sits and listens to Jesus. Martha asks Jesus to rebuke her sister for
not helping, but instead Jesus commends Mary. Regrettably, this story
has often suffered from dubious interpretations, with Martha becoming
the poster child for all that is wrong with the life of busyness and dis-
traction, or what the medieval church called the active or working life,
which was permitted but inferior to the perfect life of contemplation or
monasticism. But the story must be read against the backdrop of Luke's
Gospel as a whole, where the work of hospitality (a vital form of generosity in the ancient Near East) is one of the chief signs of the in-breaking
of God's kingdom.[6]

Mary and Martha are not enemies but sisters. Two sisters squab-
bling about household duties cannot reasonably be construed as a battle
between incompatible modes of life. Martha's generous service is not
minimized by Jesus, but her worries show that her service needs to be
grounded in Mary's kind of love for him. Together, the sisters embody
the truth that generosity and love of God are intertwined realities. Martha performs the kind of generosity Jesus commends in Luke 14:12–14,
for he is someone who cannot pay her back in kind. By sitting at Jesus'
feet, Mary shows that all our service ought to be grounded in a lively
personal relationship with him. Following Christ means becoming like
Martha and Mary. Be generous and love God. These are mutually rein-
forcing, as is the two sisters' relationship with each other.

---

[6] See Brendan Byrne, *The Hospitality of God: A Reading of Luke's Gospel*
(Collegeville, MN: Liturgical Press, 2000).

The Road to Emmaus (Luke 24:13–35)

The episode on the road to Emmaus is a fitting example of generosity for all Jesus' followers. At first it seems to take Jesus' death almost too lightly, or are we wrong to see something humorous in the two disciples instructing Jesus in the latest news? "Are you the only stranger in Jerusalem who does not know the things that have taken place there in these days?" they ask (Luke 24:18). One can almost imagine Cleopas adding, "Where have you been?" Jesus takes it in stride and lets them talk, but then turns the tide and makes them listen. Gradually, the light begins to dawn on them that perhaps the women's story of the Messiah's miraculous resurrection is not as crazy as they initially thought.

If this were all there was to the story, we might learn nothing more than that we are often "foolish . . . and . . . slow of heart to believe" (Luke 24:25) all that God has written. But the disciples do one thing right in this story—something so apparently insignificant it would be easy to miss. They offer hospitality to Jesus: "Stay with us, because it is almost evening and the day is now nearly over" (Luke 24:29). Jesus blesses this small act of generosity with the revelation of his presence. In the breaking of the bread they at last recognize him (Luke 24:32). When we offer hospitality, God uses it not only as a means of serving those in need of refreshment, but also as an invitation for us to experience Jesus' presence ourselves.

Investing in Jesus' Work (Luke 8:3; 10:7)

The parable of the shrewd manager (Luke 16:1–13) teaches the importance of using money wisely. Luke provides examples in the persons of those who invest their money in Jesus' work: Mary Magdalene, Joanna, and Susanna are named alongside the twelve disciples because of their financial support for Jesus' work. It is surprising how prominently women figure in this list, because few women in the ancient world possessed wealth. Yet "these women were helping to support them out of their own means" (Luke 8:3, NIV). Later, when Jesus sends out evangelists, he tells them to depend on the generosity of the people among whom they serve, "for the laborer deserves to be paid" (Luke 10:7).

What may seem surprising is that these two somewhat off-hand comments are all that Luke says about giving to what we would now recognize as the church. Compared to the unceasing concern Jesus shows for giving to the poor, he doesn't make much of giving to the church. Nowhere, for instance, does he interpret the Old Testament tithe as belonging to the church. This is not to say that Jesus sets generosity to the poor against generosity to the church. Instead, it is a matter of emphasis. We should note that giving money is not the only means of generosity. People also participate in God's redemptive work by creatively employing their skills, passions, relationships, and prayers.

Power and Leadership in Luke

As king, Jesus is the leader of God's realm. He employs his power in many ways recorded in the Gospel of Luke. Yet Christians are often reluctant to exercise leadership or power, as if the two were inherently evil. Jesus teaches otherwise. Christians are called to lead and to exercise power, but unlike the powers of the fallen world, they are to use it for God's purposes rather than for their own self-interest.

Persistence: The Parable of the Persistent Widow (Luke 18:1–8)

In the parable of the persistent widow (Luke 18:1–8), a poor, powerless person (the widow) persists in nagging a corrupt, powerful person (the judge) to do justice for her. The parable *assumes* John the Baptist's teaching that holding a position of power and leadership obligates you to work justly, especially on behalf of the poor and weak. But Jesus focuses the parable on a different point, that we are "to pray always and to not lose heart" (Luke 18:1). He identifies the hearers—us—with the woman, and the prayed-to person—God—with the corrupt judge, a strange combination. Assuming that Jesus doesn't mean that God is corrupt, the point must be that if persistence pays off with a corrupt human of limited power, how much more will it pay off with a just God of infinite power.

The purpose of the parable is to encourage Christians to persevere in their faith against all odds. But it also has two applications for those who work in positions of leadership. First, the juxtaposition of a corrupt judge with a just God implies that God's will is at work even in a corrupt world. The judge's job is to do justice, and by God, he *will* do justice by the time the widow is finished with him. Elsewhere, the Bible teaches that the civil authorities serve by God's authorization, whether they acknowledge it or not (John 19:11; Rom. 13:1; 1 Pet. 2:13). So there is hope that even in the midst of systemic injustice, justice may be done. A Christian leader's job is to work toward that hope at all times. We cannot right every wrong in the world in our lifetimes. But we must never give up hope, and never stop working for the greater good[7] in the midst of the imperfect systems where our work occurs. Legislators, for example, seldom have a choice of voting for a good bill versus a bad bill. Usually the best they can do is to vote for bills that do more good than bad. But they must continually look for opportunities to bring bills to a vote that do even less harm and even more good.

The second point is that only God can bring about justice in a corrupt world. That is why we must pray and not give up in our work. God can bring miraculous justice in a corrupt world, just as God can bring miraculous healing in a sick world. Suddenly, the Berlin wall opens, the apartheid regime crumbles, peace breaks out. In the parable of the persistent widow, God does not intervene. The widow's persistence alone leads the judge to act justly. But Jesus indicates that God is the unseen actor: "Will not God grant justice to his chosen ones who cry to him day and night?" (Luke 18:7).

Risk: The Parable of the Ten Minas (Luke 19:11–27)

The parable of the ten minas ("pounds" in the NRSV translation) is set in the workplace of high finance. A rich—and soon to be powerful—nobleman goes on an extended trip to be crowned king. Most of his people hate him and send word ahead that they oppose this coronation (Luke 19:14). In his absence, he assigns three of his servants to invest his money. Two of them take the risk of investing their master's money. They earn handsome returns. A third servant is afraid to take the risk, so he puts the money in a safe place. It earns no return. When the master returns,

---

[7]The use of the term "greater good" implies that the consequences of our actions are important in Christian ethics. This mode of ethical thinking, called "consequentialism," may be unfamiliar to those who are used to thinking of the Bible only in terms of ethical rules. However, the Bible makes use of all three modes of ethical reasoning that have been identified over the centuries: rules, consequences, and virtues. By no means does this make the Bible "relativistic" or "utilitarian," to name two ethical systems that truly are foreign to biblical thinking.

he has become king of the whole territory. He rewards the two servants who made money for him, promoting them to high positions of their own. He punishes the servant who kept the money safe but unproductive. Then he commands that all who opposed him be killed in his presence.

Jesus tells this parable immediately before going to Jerusalem, where he is to be crowned king ("Blessed is the king who comes in the name of the Lord," Luke 19:38) but is soon rejected by his people. This identifies Jesus with the nobleman in the parable, and the crowd shouting "Crucify him!" (Luke 23:21) with the people in the parable who oppose the nobleman's coronation. By this we know that the people have profoundly misjudged their soon-to-be king, except for the two servants who work diligently in his absence. The parable, in this context, warns us that we must decide if Jesus is indeed God's appointed king and be prepared to abide the consequences of our decision either to serve him or oppose him.[8]

This parable makes explicit that citizens of God's kingdom are responsible to work toward God's goals and purposes. In this parable, the king tells his servants directly what he expects them to do, namely, to invest his money. This specific calling or command makes it clear that preaching, healing, and evangelism (the apostles' callings) are not the only things God calls people to do. Of course, not everyone in God's kingdom is called to be an investor, either. In this parable, only three of the country's residents are called to be investors. The point is that acknowledging Jesus as king requires working toward his purposes in whatever field of work you do.

Seen in this light, the parable suggests that if we choose to accept Jesus as king, we must expect to lead risky lives. The servants who invested the master's money faced the risk of being attacked by those around them who rejected the master's authority. And they faced the risk of disappointing their master by making investments that might lose money. Even their success exposes them to risk. Now that they have tasted success and been promoted, they risk becoming greedy or power-mad. They face the risk that their next investments—which will involve much greater sums—will fail and expose them to much more severe

---

[8] Darrell L. Bock, *Luke 9:51–24:53*, Baker Exegetical Commentary on the New Testament (Grand Rapids: Baker Books, 1996), 1525–45.

consequences. In Anglo-American business (and sports) practice, CEOs (and head coaches) are routinely fired for mediocre results, whereas those in lower-level positions are fired only for exceptionally poor performance. Neither failure nor success is safe in this parable, or in today's workplace. It is tempting to duck for cover and search for a safe way of accommodating to the system while waiting for things to get better. But ducking for cover is the one action Jesus condemns in the parable. The servant who tries to avoid risk is singled out as unfaithful. We are not told what would have happened if the other two servants had lost money on their investments, but the implication is that all investments made in faithful service to God are pleasing to him, whether or not they achieve their intended payoff. (For a discussion of the highly similar parable of the talents, see "Matthew 25:14–30" in "Matthew and Work.")

Humble Service (Luke 9:46–50; 14:7–11; 22:24–30)

Jesus declares that leadership requires humble service to others, as we see in three additional passages. In the first (Luke 9:46–50), Jesus' disciples begin arguing who will be the greatest. Jesus replies that the greatest is the one who welcomes a child in his name. "The least among all of you is the greatest." Notice that the model is not the child, but the person who welcomes a child. Serving those whom everyone else considers not worth their time is what makes a leader great.

The second passage (Luke 14:7–11) is Jesus' response to the social posturing he sees at a banquet. Not only is it a waste of time, Jesus says, it's actually counterproductive. "All who exalt themselves will be humbled, and those who humble themselves will be exalted." As applied to leadership, this means that if you try to take credit for everything, people will want to stop following you, or get distracted from their work by trying to make you look bad. But if you give credit to others, people will want to follow you and that will lead to true recognition.

The third passage (Luke 22:24–30) returns to the question of who is the greatest among the disciples. This time Jesus makes himself the model of leadership through service. "I am among you as one who serves." In all three stories, the concepts of service and humility are tied together. Effective leadership requires—or *is*—service. Service requires acting as if you are less important than you think you are.

Taxing Issues (Luke 19:1–10; 20:20–26)

All along, Luke has identified Jesus as the one who is bringing God's rule to earth. In chapter 19, the people of Jerusalem finally recognize him as a king. As he rides into town on a colt, crowds line the road and sing his praises: "Blessed is the king who comes in the name of the Lord! Peace in heaven, and glory in the highest heaven!" (Luke 19:38). As we know, God's kingdom encompasses all of life, and the issues Jesus chooses to discuss immediately before and after his entry into Jerusalem touch on taxes and investments.

Zacchaeus, the Tax Collector (Luke 19:1–10)

As he passes through Jericho on his way to Jerusalem, Jesus comes upon a tax collector named Zacchaeus, who is sitting in a tree to get a better view of Jesus. "Zacchaeus, hurry and come down; for I must stay at your house today," Jesus says (Luke 19:5). The encounter with Jesus profoundly changes the way Zacchaeus works. Like all tax collectors in Roman client states, Zacchaeus made his money from overcharging people on their taxes. Although this was what we might now call "industry standard practice," it depended on deceit, intimidation, and corruption. Once Zacchaeus comes into the kingdom of God, he can no longer work this way. "Zacchaeus stood there and said to the Lord, 'Look, half of my possessions, Lord, I will give to the poor; and if I have defrauded anyone of anything, I will pay back four times as much'" (Luke 19:8). Exactly how—or whether—he will continue to make a living, he doesn't say, for it is beside the point. As a citizen of God's kingdom, he cannot engage in business practices contrary to God's ways.

Render unto God What Is God's (Luke 20:20–26)

After Jesus is welcomed as king in Jerusalem, there is a passage in Luke that has often been used wrongly to separate the world of work from the kingdom of God: Jesus' saying about taxes. The teachers of the law and the chief priests try to "trap him by what he said, so as to hand him over to the jurisdiction and authority of the governor" (Luke 20:20). They ask him whether it is lawful to pay taxes to Caesar. In response, he asks them to show him a coin, and immediately they produce a denarius. He asks whose portrait is on it and they reply, "Caesar's." Jesus says, "Then give back to Caesar what is Caesar's, and to God what is God's" (Luke 20:25, NIV).

This reply has sometimes been interpreted as separating the material from the spiritual, the political from the religious, and the earthly and from the heavenly realms. In church (God's realm), we must be honest and generous, and look after the good of our brothers and sisters. At work (Caesar's realm), we must shade the truth, be driven by worry about money, and look out for ourselves above all. But this misunderstands the sharp irony in Jesus' reply. When he says, "Give back to Caesar what is Caesar's," he is not sanctioning a separation of the material from the spiritual. The premise that Caesar's world and God's world do not overlap makes no sense in light of what Jesus has been saying throughout the Gospel of Luke. What is God's? Everything! Jesus' coming into the world as king is God's claim that the entire world is God's. Whatever may belong to Caesar also belongs to God. The world of taxes, government, production, distribution, and every other kind of work is the world that God's kingdom is breaking into. Christians are called to engage that world, not to drop out of it. This passage is the opposite of a justification of separating the work world from the Christian world. Give to Caesar what is Caesar's (taxes) and to God what is God's (everything, taxes included). (For a more thorough discussion of this incident, see the section on "Matthew 17:24–27 and 22:15–22" in "Matthew and Work.")

The Passion (Luke 22:47–24:53)

Jesus' work climaxes in his willing self-sacrifice on the cross, as with his last gasp he breathes out trust in God: "Father, into your hands I commend my spirit" (Luke 23:46). By Jesus' self-sacrifice and by the Father's mighty deed of resurrection, Jesus passes fully into the position of eternal king foretold at his birth. "The Lord God will give to him the throne of his ancestor David. He will reign over the house of Jacob *forever*" (Luke 1:32–33). This is truly God's beloved Son, faithful unto death as he works on behalf of all who have fallen into the poverty of sin and death, in need of a redemption we cannot provide ourselves. In this light, we see that Jesus' care for the poor and powerless is both an end in itself and a sign of his love for everyone who will follow him. We are *all* poor and powerless in the face of our sin and the world's brokenness. In his resurrection we find ourselves transformed in every aspect of life, as we are caught up in this extravagant love of God.

Conclusion to Luke

The Gospel of Luke is the story of the emergence of the kingdom of God on earth in the person of Jesus Christ. As the true king of the world, Christ is both the ruler to whom we owe our allegiance and the model for how we are to exercise whatever authority we are given in life.

As our ruler, he gives us one great commandment in two parts: "You shall love the Lord your God with all your heart, and with all your soul, and with all your strength, and with all your mind; and your neighbor as yourself. . . . Do this, and you will live" (Luke 10:27–28). In one sense, this commandment is nothing new. It is simply a summary of the Law of Moses. What is new is that the kingdom based on this law has been inaugurated by God's incarnation in the person of Jesus. It was God's intent from the beginning that humanity should live in this kingdom. But from the time of Adam and Eve's sin onwards, people have lived instead in the kingdom of darkness and evil. Jesus has come to reclaim the earth as God's kingdom and to create a community of God's people who live under his rule, even while the kingdom of darkness retains much of its sway. The essential response of those who come to citizenship in Christ's kingdom is that they live *all* of their lives—including work—in pursuit of the purposes and according to the ways of his kingdom.

As our model, Jesus teaches us these purposes and ways. He calls us to work at tasks such as healing, proclamation, justice, power, leadership, productivity and provision, investment, government, generosity, and hospitality. He sends God's spirit to give us everything we need to fulfill our specific callings. He promises to provide for us. He commands us to provide for others, and thereby suggests that his provision for us will generally come in the form of other people working on our behalf. He warns us of the trap of seeking self-sufficiency through wealth, and he teaches us that the best way to avoid the trap is to use our wealth in

furtherance of relationships with God and with other people. When conflicts arise in our relationships, he teaches us how to resolve them so they
lead to justice and reconciliation. Above all, he teaches that citizenship
in God's kingdom means working as a servant of God and of people. His
self-sacrifice on the cross serves as the ultimate model of servant leadership. His resurrection to the throne of God's kingdom confirms and establishes forever the active love of our neighbor as *the* way of eternal life.

JOHN AND WORK

Introduction to John

Work pervades the Gospel of John. It starts with the work of the Messiah, who is God's agent of the creation of the world. Christ's work of creation predates the Fall, predates his incarnation in the form of Jesus of Nazareth, and predates his work of redemption. He is sent by God to be the redeemer of the world precisely because he is already the co-creator of the world. His work of redemption is not a novel course of action, but a restoration of the world to the path it was always intended to take. It is a fulfillment of the creation's promise.

Human labor is an integral part of the fulfillment of creation (Gen. 2:5). But the work humans do has become corrupted, so the redemption of *work* is an integral part of the Messiah's redemption of the world. During his earthly ministry, we will see that the work Jesus does for the Father is an integral aspect of Father and Son's love for each other. "The words that I say to you I do not speak on my own; but the Father who dwells in me does his works" (John 14:10). This provides the model for redeemed human labor, which is likewise meant to nurture our love for one another as we work together in God's good world. In addition to modeling good work, Jesus teaches about workplace topics such as calling, relationships, creativity and productivity, ethics, truth and deception, leadership, service, sacrifice and suffering, and the dignity of labor.

One of John's chief interests is to remind people that a casual glance at Jesus will never do. Those who remain with him find his simple images opening up into an entirely new way of looking at the world. This is as true of work as it is of anything else. The Greek word for "work" (*ergon*) appears over twenty-five times in the Gospel, while the more general term for "doing" (*poieō*) occurs over one hundred times. In most cases, the words refer to Jesus' work for the Father; but even this, it turns out, will hold promise for ordinary human employment. The key to making sense of this material is that it takes work to work out what the Gospel of John means. The meaning often lies deeper than a casual reading can uncover. Therefore, we will delve into a limited number of passages with particular meaning for work, workers, and workplaces. We will pass over passages that do not contribute essentially to our topic.

The Word's Work in the World (John 1:1–18)

"In the beginning was the Word, and the Word was with God, and the Word was God. He was in the beginning with God. All things came into being through him, without him not one thing came into being." The majestic opening of John's Gospel shows us the limitless scope of the Word's work. He is the definitive self-expression of God, the one through whom God created *all things* in the beginning. He stretches out the cosmos as the canvas for the expression of God's glory.

The Word is working; and because his work began in the beginning, all subsequent human labor is derived from his initial labor. *Derived* is not too strong a word, because everything people work with was created by him. The work God did in Genesis 1 and 2 was performed *by* the Word. This may seem too fine a point to press, but many Christians continue to labor under the delusion that the Messiah only began working once things had gone irredeemably wrong, and that his work is restricted to saving (invisible) souls to bring them to (immaterial) heaven. Once we recognize that the Messiah was working materially with God from the beginning, we can reject every creation-denying (and thus work-denigrating) theology.

Therefore we need to correct a common misunderstanding. John's Gospel is *not* grounded in a dichotomy of the spiritual versus the material, or the sacred versus the profane, or any other dualism. It does not portray salvation as the liberation of the human spirit from the shackles of the material body. Dualistic philosophies such as these are regrettably common among Christians. Their proponents have often turned to the language of the Gospel of John to support their views. It is true that John frequently records Jesus' use of contrasts such as light/darkness (John 1:5; 3:19; 8:12; 11:9–10; 12:35–36), belief/unbelief (John 3:12–18; 4:46–54; 5:46–47; 10:25–30; 12:37–43; 14:10–11; 20:24–31) and spirit/

flesh (John 3:6–7). These contrasts highlight the conflict between God's ways and the ways of evil. But they do not constitute a division of the universe into dual sub-universes. They certainly do not call Jesus' followers to abandon some sort of "secular" world in order to enter a "spiritual" one. Instead, Jesus employs the contrasts to call his followers to receive and use the power of God's spirit in the present world. Jesus states this directly in John 3:17: "God did not send the Son into the world to condemn the world, but in order that the world might be saved through him." Jesus came to restore the world to the way God intended it to be, not to lead an exodus out of the world.

If further evidence for God's ongoing commitment to the creation is needed, we may turn to John 1:14: "The Word became flesh and lived among us." The incarnation is not the triumph of the spirit over the flesh, but the fulfillment of what the flesh was created for in the beginning. And the flesh is not a temporary base of operations, but the Word's permanent abode. After his resurrection, Jesus invites Thomas and the others to touch his flesh (John 20:24–31) and later has a breakfast of fish with them (John 21:1–14). At the end of the Gospel, Jesus tells his disciples to wait "until I return" (John 21:22–23, NIV), not "until I get us all out of here." A God hostile to, or uninterested in, the material realm would hardly be inclined to take up permanent residence within it. If the world in general is of such immense concern to God, it stands to reason that the work done within that world matters to him as well.

Calling Disciples/Friends (John 1:35–51)

We will return to the conventional term "disciples" momentarily, but the term "friends" captures the essence of John's depiction of the disciples. "I have called you friends," says Jesus (John 15:15). The relational element is critical: they are Jesus' friends who first and foremost remain in his presence (John 1:35–39; 11:54; 15:4–11). John appears to go out of his way to crowd as many people as possible onstage with Jesus in chapter 1. John the Baptist points Jesus out to Andrew and another disciple. Andrew gets his brother Simon. Philip, who is from the same town as Andrew and Simon, finds Nathanael. It is not simply that Jesus will advance his mission *through* a web of interpersonal relationships. Weaving a web of relationships *is the point* of the whole enterprise.

But the disciples are not just buddies basking in the radiance of Jesus' friendship. They are also his workers. They are not working in an obvious way yet in chapter 1 (though even the fetching of siblings and neighbors is a type of evangelistic labor), but work they will. Indeed, as we will see, it is precisely this connection between friendship and labor that holds the key to John's theology of work. Work produces results while it also builds relationships, and this is another echo of Genesis 2:18–22.

The Wedding Planner (John 2:1–11)

Jesus' "first sign" (John 2:11), changing water into wine, lays the foundation for understanding the subsequent signs. This is no parlor trick done to attract attention to himself. He does it reluctantly, and the miracle is hidden even from the master of the banquet. Jesus does it only in the face of pressing human need and to honor his mother's request. (Running out of wine at the wedding would have brought great shame on the bride, the groom, and their families, and that shame would have lingered long in the village culture of Cana.) Far from being an unmoved mover (as some Greeks regarded God), Jesus shows himself to be the loving, responsive Son of the loving, eternal Father and the beloved human mother.

The fact that he turns the water to wine shows that he is like the Father not only in love, but also in his power over the creation. Attentive readers of John should not be surprised that the Word who made all things, now made flesh himself, is able to bring material blessings to his people. To deny that Jesus can work miracles would be to deny that Christ was with God in the beginning. What is most surprising, perhaps, is that this apparently unplanned miracle ends up pointing unmistakably to Jesus' ultimate purpose. He has come to draw people to God's consummate wedding feast, where they will joyfully dine with him together. Jesus' mighty works, done with the stuff of the present world order, are amazing blessings in the here and now; and they also point to still greater blessings in the world to come.

Jesus' Hand in All Things (John 3:1–36)

Jesus' discussions with Nicodemus and his disciples hold innumerable treasures. We will begin with a verse that has profound implications for human labor: "The Father loves the Son and has placed all things in his hands" (John 3:35). While the immediate context emphasizes the fact that the Son speaks the Father's words, the remainder of the Gospel makes it clear that "all things" really does mean "all things." God has authorized his Messiah to create all things, God sustains all things through him, and God will bring all things to their appointed goal through him.

This passage reiterates what we learned in the prologue: the Father involves the Son in the founding and sustaining of the world. What is new is the revelation of *why* the Father chose to include the Son, rather than simply creating by himself. It was an act of love. The Father shows his love for the Son by placing all things in his hands, beginning with the act of creation. The world is a "labor of love" in the fullest sense of the word. Work must be something more wonderful than we usually give it credit for if *adding* to someone's workload is an act of love. We will develop this all-important idea further as we see Jesus in action throughout the remainder of the Gospel.

But chapter 3 does more than reiterate how the Word took on human flesh. It also illustrates the inverse process, how human flesh can become filled with God's Spirit. "Very truly, I tell you, no one can enter the kingdom of God without being born of water and Spirit" (John 3:5). We receive God's Spirit ("enter his kingdom") through a form of *birth*. Birth is a process that occurs in the flesh. When we become truly spiritual, we do not slough off the flesh and enter some immaterial state. Instead, we are more perfectly born—born "from above" (John 3:3)—into a state of union of Spirit and flesh, like Jesus himself.

During his discussion with Nicodemus, Jesus says that those born from above will "come to the light, so that it may be clearly seen that their deeds have been done in God" (John 3:21). Later he uses the metaphor of *walking* in the light to illustrate the same idea (John 8:12; 11:9–10; 12:35–36). This has important ethical implications for work. If we are conducting all our work openly, we have a powerful tool for remaining faithful to the ethics of God's kingdom. But if we find ourselves hiding

or obscuring our work, it is often a strong indication that we are following an unethical path. This is not an unbending rule, for Jesus himself
acted in secret at times (John 7:10), as did his followers, such as Joseph
of Arimathea (John 19:38). But at the least we might ask, "Who is my
secrecy truly protecting?"

For example, consider a man heading a business in mission in Africa that builds boats for use on Lake Victoria. He says he is frequently
approached by local officials who want him to pay a bribe. The request
is always made in secret. It is not a documented, open payment, as is
a tip or an expediting fee for faster service. There are no receipts and
the transaction is not recorded anywhere. He has used John 3:20–21 as
an inspiration to draw these requests into the light. He will say to the
official requesting the bribe, "I don't know much about these kinds of
payments. I would like to bring in the ambassador, or the management,
to get this documented." He has found this to be a helpful strategy for
dealing with bribery.

It is important to understand that the metaphor of walking in the
light is not a one-size-fits-all rule. Confidentiality and secrecy can have
a proper place in work, as in personnel matters, online privacy, or trade
secrets. But even if we deal with information that should not be made
public, we seldom need to act in complete darkness. If we are hiding our
actions from others in our departments or from people with a legitimate
interest, or if we would be ashamed to see them reported in the news,
then we may have a good indication that we are acting unethically.

Water Works (John 4)

The story of the woman at the well (John 4:1–40) has as much direct
discussion of human labor as any story in John; but one has to draw
deeply to taste it all. Many Christians are familiar with the woman's
inability to move from the everyday work of drawing water to Jesus'
pronouncements on the life-giving power of his word. This motif perme-
ates the Gospel: the crowds repeatedly show an inability to transcend
everyday concerns and address the spiritual aspects of life. They do not
see how Jesus can offer them his body as bread (John 6:51–61). They
think they know where he is from (Nazareth, John 1:45–46), but they fail

to see where he is really from (heaven); and they are equally ignorant as to where he is going (John 14:1–6).

All of this is certainly relevant for thinking about work. Whatever we think of the intrinsic good of a steady water supply (and every drink we take confirms that it is indeed a good thing!), this story surely tells us that physical water alone cannot confer on us eternal life. In addition, it is easy for modern Westerners to miss the drudgery of the woman's daily water chores, and ascribe her reluctance to fetch the water to sheer laziness. But the curse on labor (Gen. 3:14–19) bites hard, and she can be forgiven for wanting a more efficient delivery system.

We should not conclude, however, that Jesus comes to free us from work in the grimy material world so that we can bathe in the sublime waters of spiritual serenity. We must first, as always, remember the comprehensive nature of Christ's work as depicted in John 1: the Messiah made the water in the well, and he made it good. If he then uses that water to illustrate the dynamics of the Spirit's work in the hearts of would-be worshippers, that could be seen as an *ennoblement* of the water rather than a downgrading of it. The fact that we reckon first with the Creator, then with the creation, is no slight on the creation, especially since one function of creation is to point us toward the Creator.

We see something similar in the aftermath of the story, where Jesus uses reaping as a metaphor to help the disciples understand their mission in the world:

> "Do you not say, 'Four months more, then comes the harvest'? But I tell you, look around you, and see how the fields are ripe for harvesting. The reaper is already receiving wages and is gathering fruit for eternal life, so that sower and reaper may rejoice together." (John 4:35–36)

In addition to providing the palpable blessing of the daily bread for which we are instructed to pray, agricultural work can *also* serve as a way of understanding the advance of God's kingdom.

More than that, Jesus directly dignifies labor in this passage. We first have the statement, "My food is to do the will of him who sent me and to complete his work [Gk. *ergon*]" (John 4:34). It is worth noting that the first appearance of the Greek word *ergon* in the Bible[1] shows

---

[1] That is, in the Septuagint, the ancient Greek translation of the Hebrew Bible.

up in Genesis 2:2: "On the seventh day God finished the work [Gk. "his works," *erga*] that he had done, and he rested on the seventh day from all the work that he had done [again, "his works," *erga* in Gk.]." While we cannot be certain that Jesus is alluding to this verse in Genesis, it makes sense in light of the rest of the Gospel to take "God's work" in John 4:34 to mean the comprehensive restoration or completion of the work God had done in the beginning.

There is something more subtle at work here as well. In John 4:38, Jesus makes the somewhat cryptic statement, "I sent you to reap that for which you did not labor. Others have labored, and you have entered into their labor." He is referring to the fact that the disciples have a field of Samaritans ripe for the kingdom, if they will only open their eyes to the opportunity. But who are the "others" who have done the "labor"? Part of the answer seems to be, surprisingly, the woman at the well, who is remembered more for her spiritual slowness than for her subsequent effective testimony for Jesus: "Many Samaritans from that city believed in him because of the woman's testimony, 'He told me everything I have ever done'" (John 4:39). The disciples will simply be reaping where the woman has sown. Yet there is still another worker here: Christ himself. Back at the beginning of the story, we read that Jesus was "tired" from his journey. A more literal translation would be that Jesus was "labored" from his journey. The word translated "tired" is *kekopiakōs*, literally "labored." This is the same root that appears in John 4:38 (and nowhere else in John's Gospel): ". . . you did not labor [*kekopiakate*] . . . others have labored [*kekopiakasin*] . . . you have entered into their labor [*kopon*] . . ." In truth, Jesus was labored from his journey in Samaria. The field of Samaria is ripe for harvest in part because Christ has labored there. Whatever work we do as Christ's followers is filled with the glory of God, because Christ has already worked the same fields to prepare them for us.

As we have seen, the redemptive work of Christ after the Fall is of a kind with his creative/productive work from the beginning of time. Likewise, the redemptive work of his followers is in the same sphere as the creative/productive work typified by homemakers drawing water and farmers reaping crops.

Evangelism is one of the many forms of human work, neither higher nor lower than homemaking or farming. It is a distinctive form of work, and nothing else can substitute for it. The same may be said of drawing water and harvesting grain. Evangelism does not displace creative/productive work to become the only truly worthy human activity, particularly since any work well done by Christians is a testimony to the renewing power of the Creator.

Who Works When, and Why? (John 5)

The healing of the man at the pool of Bethsaida brings to the surface a controversy familiar from Matthew, Mark, and Luke: Jesus' penchant for healing on the Sabbath. If the controversy is familiar, however, Jesus' self-defense takes a slightly different angle in John's Gospel. His lengthy argument is crisply summarized in John 5:17: "My Father is still working, and I also am working." The principle is clear. God keeps the creation going even on the Sabbath, and therefore Jesus, who shares the divine identity, is permitted to do the same. Jesus was almost certainly not alone in arguing that God was at work on the Sabbath, but his deduction justifying his own work is unique.

As a result, we cannot use this story to deduce the propriety or impropriety of *our* working on the Sabbath. We may be doing God's work, but we do not share the divine identity as Christ does. Human work having life-or-death consequences—military self-defense (1 Macc. 2:41) or pulling an animal from a ditch—was already accepted as legitimate on the Sabbath. The healing itself is not questioned in this episode, even though the man would have suffered no harm had Jesus waited until Sunday to heal him. Instead, Jesus is criticized for permitting him to carry a mat—a form of work, according to the Jewish Law—on the Sabbath. Does this imply that Jesus permits us to drive to vacation on the Sabbath? Fly on Sunday to a business meeting that begins on Monday morning? Operate a continuous casting plant 24/7/365? There is no hint here that Jesus is merely widening the list of activities permitted on the Sabbath. Instead, let us apply the theme we see running through John—work that maintains and redeems the creation (material or spiritual), and contributes to closer relationships with God and people, is appropriate for the Sabbath. Whether any particular work fulfills this description must be discerned by the person(s) involved. (For more on this topic, see "Matthew 12:1–8" in "Matthew and Work," "Mark 1:21–45" and "Mark 2:23–3:6" in "Mark and Work," and "Luke 6:1–11; 13:10–17" in "Luke and Work.")

A clearer, and more important, lesson for us from this narrative is that God is still at work to maintain the present creation, and Jesus furthers that work in his healing ministry. Jesus' signs are at one level the in-breaking of the new world. They demonstrate "the powers of the age to come" (Heb. 6:5). At the same time, they are also the up-keeping of the present world. It seems perfectly appropriate to see this as a paradigm for our own myriad jobs. As we act in faith to restore what has been broken (as doctors, nurses, auto mechanics, and so forth), we call people to remember the goodness of the creator God. As we act in faith to develop the capacities of the creation (as programmers, teachers, artists, and so on), we call people to reflect on the goodness of humanity's God-given dominion over the world. The work of redemption and the work of creation/production, done in faith, both shout out our trust in the God who is, and who was, and who is to come. God created all things through Christ, is restoring them to his original intent through Christ, and will bring them to their appointed goal through Christ.

Bread of Life (John 6)

John's telling of the feeding of the five thousand (John 6:1–15) echoes many of the themes we saw in the wedding feast at Cana and the healing of the paralytic man. Again, Jesus works to sustain life in the present world, even as the sign points toward the ultimate life he alone can offer. John 6:27–29, however, poses a particular challenge for the theology of work:

> "Do not work for the food that perishes, but for the food that endures for eternal life, which the Son of Man will give you. For it is on him that God the Father has set his seal." Then they said to him, "What must we do to perform the works of God?" Jesus answered them, "This is the work of God, that you believe in him whom he has sent."

A quick reading reveals at least two major issues: first, Jesus appears to issue a direct command not to work; and second, he appears to reduce even work for God to belief.

The first issue is fairly easy to address. All Scripture, like all communication, must be seen in context. The issue in John 6 is that people want to keep Jesus around to serve as a Magical Baker King, who will keep the loaves coming. Thus when Jesus says, "You are looking for me, not because you saw signs, but because you ate your fill of the loaves" (John 6:26), he is rebuking their spiritual shortsightedness. They ate the bread, but they were unable to see what this sign signified. It is the same lesson we learned in chapter 4. Eternal life comes not from an unending supply of food, but from the living Word who proceeds from the mouth of God. Jesus ceases the preliminary work (serving loaves) when it no longer results in the desired end product (relationship with God). Any competent worker would do the same. If adding more salt ceases to make the soup taste better, a decent cook stops adding salt. Jesus doesn't mean "stop working," but stop working for more stuff (food) when more stuff isn't what you need. This may sound too obvious to need the Word of God to tell us, but who among us doesn't need to hear that truth again this very day? The apparent prohibition against working for temporal gain is a hyperbolic expression designed to focus on mending the crowd's relationship to God.

As for the issue of work being reduced simply to belief, this must be seen against the backdrop of the rest of the Gospel and the theology of John's letters. John delights in pushing things to extremes. On the one hand, his high view of God's sovereignty and creative power leads him to exalt a humble dependence on God, as we see in this chapter. God's work on our behalf is infinite—we need only to believe him and accept the work of God in Christ. On the other hand, Jesus is equally capable of laying the emphasis on our active obedience: "Whoever says, 'I abide in him,' ought to walk just as he walked" (1 John 2:6), and again, "The love of God is this, that we *obey* his commandments" (1 John 5:3). We might join these two extremes with the Pauline expression, "the obedience of faith" (Rom. 1:5), or James 2:18, "I by my works will show you my faith."

Seeing and Believing (John 9)

Jesus and his disciples see a man born blind (chapter 9). The disciples look on him as a lesson or case study on the sources of sin. Jesus looks on him with compassion and works to remedy his condition. Christ's unusual method of healing and the subsequent actions of the no-longer-blind man again show that the world of flesh and blood—and mud—is the place of God's kingdom. Jesus' method—mixing spit with dirt and putting it on the man's eyes—is not madness, but a calculated echo of the creation of mankind (Gen. 2:7). In both biblical and Greek tradition, mud (*pēlos*) is used to describe what people are made of. Note, for example, Job 10:9, where Job says to God, "Remember that you fashioned me like clay; and will you turn me to dust again?"[2]

Life, and Looming Death (John 10–12)

As Jesus draws near to Jerusalem for the last time, he does his greatest sign—the raising of Lazarus at Bethany (John 11:1–44). Jesus' opponents, who have already tried to stone him (John 8:59; 10:31), decide that both Jesus and Lazarus must go. With his death looming, Jesus speaks about the cross in a paradoxical way. He uses what appears to be the language of exaltation, saying that he will be "lifted up" and draw all people to himself (John 12:32). Yet John makes clear in the follow-up note that this refers to the "lifting up" of the cross. Is this mere wordplay? Not at all. As Richard Bauckham points out, it is in the work of supreme self-sacrifice on the cross that Jesus fully reveals that he is indeed the exalted Son of God. "Because God is who God is in his gracious self-giving, God's identity, we can say, is not simply revealed but enacted in the event of salvation for the world which the service and self-humiliation of his Son accomplishes."[3]

---

[2] This verse is especially interesting because the "clay" is in synonymous parallelism with dust, using the same Hebrew word for dust as in the creation of Adam in Genesis 2:7. For other associations of humanity and mud in the Bible, see, e.g., Isaiah 29:16; 45:9; Jeremiah 18:6; Sirach 33:13; Romans 9:21; cf. also Job 33:6; outside the Bible, see, e.g., Aristophanes, *Birds* 686; Herodas, *Mimes* 2.29.

[3] Richard J. Bauckham, *God Crucified: Monotheism and Christology in the New Testament* (Grand Rapids: Eerdmans, 1999), 68.

Jesus' coming self-sacrifice would extract many forms of cost. It would cost him his death, of course, but also excruciating pain and thirst (John 19:28). It cost him the heartbreak of seeing his disciples (except John) desert him and his mother bereft of him (John 19:26–27). It cost him the shame of being misunderstood and wrongly blamed (John 18:19–24). These costs were unavoidable if he was to do the work God set before him. The world could not come into being without the work of Christ in the beginning. The world could not be restored to God's intention without the work of Christ on the cross.

Our work may also call for costs that are not fair to us, but which cannot be avoided if we are to complete our work. Jesus worked to bring true life to others. To the extent that we use our work as an arena for self-glorification, we depart from the pattern set for us by the Lord Jesus. Is Jesus acknowledging that work performed for others has an unavoidable cost? Perhaps so. Doctors earn a good salary from healing people (at least in the modern West) yet suffer an unavoidable burden of pain from witnessing their patients' suffering. Plumbers get an enviable hourly rate, but also get covered with excrement from time to time. Elected officials work for justice and prosperity for their citizens, but like Jesus, bear the sorrow of knowing, "you always have the poor with you" (John 12:8). In each of these professions, there might be ways to avoid suffering alongside others—minimizing interaction with unsedated patients; plumbing only in new, unsoiled houses; or hardening our hearts to the most vulnerable people in society. Would doing so be following the pattern of Jesus? Although we often speak of work as how you make your living, any compassionate worker also experiences work as how you break your heart. In this way, we work like Jesus.

Servant Leadership (John 13)

Up to this point in John, we have seen Jesus doing work that no one else had ever done before—making water into wine, giving sight to the blind, raising the dead. Now he does what almost anyone can do, but what few want to. He washes feet. The king does the work of a slave.

In doing so, Jesus brings to a head the question that has been following us through the entire course of John's Gospel—to what extent is

Jesus' work an example for our own work? It would be easy to answer, "Not at all." None of us are the Lord. None of us die for the sins of the world. But when he washes the disciples' feet, Jesus explicitly tells them—and by extension us—that we *are* to follow his example. "So if I, your Lord and Teacher, have washed your feet, you also ought to wash one another's feet. For I have set you an example" (John 13:14–15). Jesus *is* an example we are meant to follow, so far as we are able.

This attitude of humble service should accompany all we do. If the CEO walks the production floor, it should be as if coming to wash the assembly workers' feet. So, too, the gas station attendant should clean the bathroom floors as if being there to wash the motorists' feet. This is not so much a matter of action as attitude. Both the CEO and the gas station attendant can probably serve people better through other activities than washing feet, even if their employees or customers were willing. But they should see themselves as performing humble service. Jesus, the Spirit-filled teacher who reigns over the entire cosmos, deliberately performs a concrete act of lowly service to demonstrate what ought to be the habitual attitude of his people. By doing so, he both dignifies and demands from his followers humble acts of service. Why? Because doing so brings us tangibly face to face with the reality that godly work is performed for the benefit of others, not merely for our own fulfillment.

The concept of servant leadership has received widespread attention in business and government in recent years. It arises not only in the Gospel of John but also in many parts of the Bible.[4]

Farewell Words (John 14–17)

Chapters 14 through 17, often called the Upper Room Discourse, contain so much profound theology that we can only touch on a few salient points. But it is important to recognize that Jesus' words are not a dispassionate lecture. He is in anguish for the disciples whom he loves

---

[4] Other resources include *Servant Leadership* by Robert Greenleaf (Mahwah, NJ: Paulist Press, 1977), and *Leadership Is an Art* by Max De Pree (New York: Doubleday, 1992).

and whom he must soon leave, and his words are designed above all to comfort them in their distress.

Work and Relationships (John 14–17)

An emphasis on personal relationships suffuses the theology of these chapters. Jesus tells the disciples, "I do not call you servants any longer . . . but I have called you friends" (John 15:15). They work for him, but in a spirit of friendship and collegiality. It is in the fullest sense of the term a family business. The work and the relationships intertwine, for Jesus is not working on his own. "The words that I say to you I do not speak on my own; but the Father who dwells in me does his works. Believe me that I am in the Father and the Father is in me" (John 14:10–11). Neither will the disciples be left as orphans to muddle through the world as best they can (John 14:18). Through the Spirit, Jesus will be with them, and they will do the same things he has been doing (John 14:12).

This is deeper than it may appear. It does not mean merely that after Jesus dies, his disciple/friends can still experience him in prayer. It means that they are active participants in the world-creation/restoration that fuels the loving relationship between the Father and the Son. They do the work of the Son and Father, and they join the intimacy of the Son and Father (and the Spirit, as we shall see in a moment). The Father shows his love for the Son by allowing him to share in the glory of world formation and re-creation.[5] The Son shows his love for the Father by ever and only doing his will, making and remaking the world for the Father's glory according to the Father's wishes in the power of the Spirit. The disciple/friends enter into this ever-flowing love of the Father, Son, and Spirit, not only by mystical reflection but also by embracing the Son's mission and working as he did. The call to share in the love is inextricable from the call to share in the labor. The Son's prayer, "I in them and you in me, that they may become completely one" (John 17:23),

---

[5] Cf. John 3:35, 5:19–20. The statement in John 17:5, "So now, Father, glorify me in your own presence with the glory that I had in your presence before the world existed," may well refer specifically to the glory of sharing in world formation. This would form a fitting bookend to the inclusion of Christ in the primal creation in John 1:1–3.

is matched by, "As you have sent me into the world, so I have sent them into the world" (John 17:18), and it issues forth in "Do you love me? . . . Feed my sheep" (John 21:17).

An essential aspect of human labor is the opportunity it provides for fellowship through common projects. For many people, the workplace provides the most significant context outside family for personal relationships. Even those who work alone—inside or outside their own homes—are typically enmeshed in a web of relationships involving suppliers, customers, and so on.[6] We have seen that Jesus calls his disciples not only as co-laborers but also as a community of friends. The relational aspect of work is not an accidental by-product of an essentially utilitarian enterprise of labor. Rather, it is an absolutely critical component of work itself, going back to the time when Adam and Eve worked together in the garden. "Then the LORD God said, 'It is not good that the man should be alone; I will make him a helper as his partner'" (Gen. 2:18). The creation becomes the means of interpersonal connection as humans work alongside one another, and in so doing enter into God's labor to bring creation to its fulfillment.

This can be a tremendous encouragement to project-oriented people who are sometimes made to feel unspiritual because of their reluctance to spend an abundance of time talking about their feelings. Talking with other people is a necessary activity for developing relationships, but we should not neglect the importance of doing work as a means for nurturing relationships. Working together can build relationships in and of itself. It is no accident that we spend a great deal of time working with and for other people. Modeled on God's own work within the Trinity, we are able to find *relationship in work*. Work toward a common goal is one of the chief ways God brings us together and makes us truly human.

Work and Productivity (John 14–17)

The metaphor of vine and branches begins with the blessing of relationship with Jesus and through him with the Father (John 15:1). "As

---

[6] Expressed beautifully, for example, in Robert Frost's "The Tuft of Flowers" with the memorable lines, "'Men work together,' I told him from the heart, 'Whether they work together or apart.'" Robert Frost, *A Boy's Will* (New York: Henry Holt, 1915), 49.

the Father has loved me, so I have loved you; abide in my love" (John 15:9). Yet the outcome of this love is not passive bliss but productive labor, metaphorically expressed as bearing fruit. "Those who abide in me and I in them bear much fruit" (John 15:5). The God who produced the universe wants his people to be productive too. "My Father is glorified by this, that you bear much fruit" (John 15:8). Our ability to do work that makes a lasting difference in the world is a great gift from God. "I appointed you to go and bear fruit, fruit that will last, so that the Father will give you whatever you ask him in my name" (John 15:16). The promise of effectiveness echoes Jesus' earlier promise that "the one who believes in me will also do the works that I do and, in fact, will do greater works than these" (John 14:12).

The fruit borne by Jesus' followers is sometimes taken to refer to converts to Christianity. "Greater works than these" would then mean "more converts than I myself made." For those called to evangelism, this is certainly true. If Jesus is speaking in this passage only to the apostles—appointed as they were to preach the good news—then perhaps fruit refers only to converts. But if he is speaking to believers in general, then fruit must refer to the whole range of work to which believers are called. Since the entire world was created through him, "the works that I do" include every imaginable kind of good work. For us to do "greater works" than heretofore seen could mean designing better software, feeding more people, educating wiser students, improving the effectiveness of organizations, increasing customer satisfaction, employing capital more productively, and governing nations more justly. The value of bearing fruit does not lie in whether we work in business, government, health care, education, religion, or any other field. The value lies in whether our work serves people's needs. "I am giving you these commands so that you may love one another" (John 15:17). Service is the active form of love.

Stranger in a Strange Land (John 18–20)

Rather than risk reducing John's passion narrative to a proof-text for work issues, we will address a single verse that is as important for what it does not say as for what it says: "Jesus answered [Pilate], 'My kingdom is not from this world. If my kingdom were from this world, my followers would be fighting to keep me from being handed over to the Jews. But as it is, my kingdom is not from here'" (John 18:36). On the positive side, we find here a marvelous summary of the Passion. Jesus is proclaiming that he is indeed a king, but not the sort of king who is liable to be recognized by a wily politico like Pilate. If Jesus must sacrifice himself for the life of the world, he will do so. And he must indeed sacrifice himself, because his kingship, which is both absolute and absolutely self-giving, will inevitably draw a death sentence from the powers that be.

But it is equally important to recognize what Jesus is not proclaiming. He is not saying that his kingdom is an ephemeral, internal religious experience that does not impinge on economic, political, or social issues in the real world. As the NRSV, the NIV, and other translations indicate, his kingdom is instead *from* another realm (John 18:36). His rule—like he himself—originates *from* heaven. But he has come *to* earth, and his kingdom is a real kingdom on this earth, more real than even Rome could ever be. His kingdom come to earth has a different set of operating principles. It is powerfully at work *within* the world, but it does not receive its marching orders *from the present rulers* of the world. Jesus doesn't explain at the time what it means for his kingdom to be *from* another world yet *in* the world he himself constructed. But he reveals it in vivid terms later, in the vision reported in Revelation 21 and 22, when the New Jerusalem comes down out of heaven. Jesus' kingdom descends to take its rightful place as the capital of this world, where all his disciples find their eternal home. Whenever Jesus speaks of eternal life or the kingdom of God, he is referring to the earth we inhabit now, transformed and perfected by the Word and the power of God.

Beloved Disciples (John 21)

The final chapter of John provides an opportunity to reflect not so much on work itself, but on the identity of the worker. The disciples are fishing when they meet Jesus. This is sometimes seen as a bad thing, as if they are fishing when they ought to be preaching the kingdom of God. But there is nothing in the text that suggests disapproval. Rather, Jesus blesses their labor with a miraculous catch. Afterwards, they return to their appointed work as preachers, yet even this reflects only their specific calling and is no slight on fishing as such.

However we take the setting, the impetus of the chapter is the restoration of Peter and the contrast of his future with that of the "disciple whom Jesus loved" (John 21:20). Peter's threefold affirmation of his love for Jesus restores his relationship with Jesus after his earlier threefold denial. Looking to the future, Peter will endure martyrdom, while it is cryptically hinted that the Beloved Disciple will enjoy a longer life. We will focus our attention on the latter figure, since his self-designation speaks directly to the question of human identity.

It is a curious thing that the identity of the Beloved Disciple is never revealed in the Fourth Gospel. Most scholars deduce that he is the Apostle John (though there are some dissenters[7]), but the real question is why he shrouds his name in such secrecy. One answer would be that he wishes to distinguish himself from other disciples. He is specially loved by Jesus. But this would be a strange motive in a Gospel permeated with Christ's model of humility and self-sacrifice.

A far better explanation is that he terms himself the "disciple whom Jesus loved" as a way of representing what is true of *all* disciples. We are all to find our identity first and foremost in the fact that Jesus loves us. When you ask John who he is, he does not answer by giving his name, his family connections, or his occupation. He responds, "I am someone Jesus loves." In John's words, the Beloved Disciple finds himself "leaning on Jesus' bosom" (John 13:23, KJV), and likewise, the Messiah finds his identity "in the bosom of the Father" (John 1:18, KJV).[8] In the same way, we are to find out who we are, not in what we have done, or in who we know, or in what we have, but in Jesus' love for us.

Yet if Jesus' love for us—or, we may say, the Father's love for us through Jesus—is the source of our identity and motivation of our lives, we work out this love in our activity in God's creation. One crucial aspect

---

[7] D. A. Carson, *The Gospel According to John*, The Pillar New Testament Commentary (Grand Rapids: Eerdmans, 1991), 68–81.

[8] These are the only two occurrences of "bosom," Gk. *kolpos*, in John's Gospel. We have used the King James Version because most modern translations (NASB excepted) miss this parallelism.

of that activity is our daily work. Through God's grace, work can become an arena where we live out our relationship with God and others through loving service. Our everyday labor, however humble or exalted it may be in others' estimation, becomes the place where *God's* glory is displayed. By God's grace, as we work, we become living parables of the love and glory of God.

ACTS AND WORK

Introduction to Acts

The Acts of the Apostles depicts the early church working hard to grow itself and serve others in the face of opposition, shortages of people and money, government bureaucracy (church bureaucracy came later), internal strife, and even the forces of nature. Their work shows similarities to what Christians face in non-church-related workplaces today. A small group of people put all their heart into work that brings Christ's love to people in every sphere of life, and they find the amazing power of the Holy Spirit at work in them as they do it. If this is not what we experience in our daily work, perhaps God wants to guide, gift, and empower our work as much as he did theirs.

Work takes center stage, as you might expect in a book about the "acts" of the leaders of the early church. The narrative is abuzz with people walking, speaking, healing, giving generously, making decisions, governing, serving food, managing money, fighting, manufacturing clothes, tents, and other goods, baptizing (or washing), debating, arguing, making judgments, reading and writing, singing, defending themselves in court, gathering wood, building fires, escaping hostile crowds, embracing and kissing, holding councils, apologizing, sailing, abandoning ship, swimming, rescuing people, and through it all, praising God. The men and women in the book of Acts are ready to do whatever it might take to accomplish their mission. No work is too menial for the highest among them, and no work too daunting for the lowliest.

Yet the depth of the book of Acts stems not so much from what the people of the early church do, but why and how they engage in this amazing burst of activity. The *why* is service. Serving God, serving colleagues, serving society, serving strangers—service is the motivation behind the work Christians do throughout the book. This should come as no surprise because Acts is in fact the second volume of the story that began in the Gospel of Luke, and service is also the driving motivation of Jesus and his followers in Luke. (See "Luke and Work" for essential background information on Luke and his audience.)

If the *why* is service, then the *how* is to constantly challenge the structures of Roman society, which was based not on service but exploitation. Luke continually contrasts the ways of God's kingdom with the ways of the Roman Empire. He pays attention to Jesus' and his followers' many interactions with the officials of the empire. He is well aware of the systems of power—and the socioeconomic factors that support them—operative in the Roman Empire. From the emperor to nobles, to officials, to landowners, to freemen, to servants and slaves, each layer of society existed by wielding power over the layer below. God's way, as seen in the Gospel of Luke and the book of Acts, is just the opposite. God's society exists for service, and especially for service to those in weaker, poorer, or more vulnerable positions.

Ultimately, then, Acts is not a model of the kinds of activities we should engage in as Christ's followers, but a model of the commitment to service that should form the foundation of our activities. Our activities are different from the apostles', but our commitment to service is the same.

The Beginning of God's New World (Acts 1–4)

A Community with a Mission (Acts 1:6)

In the book of Acts, Jesus' mission to restore the world as God intended it to be is transformed into the mission of the community of Jesus' followers. Acts traces the life of the community of Jesus' followers as the Spirit forms them into a group of people who work and use work-related power and wealth differently from the world around them. The work begins with the creation of the unique community called the church. Luke begins with the community "when they had come together" and continues with the mission to "restore the kingdom to Israel" (Acts 1:6). To accomplish this work, the community must first be oriented to its vocation for the kingdom of God, and then to its identity as the kingdom of God's witnesses in daily life.

An Orienting Vocation for the Kingdom of God (Acts 1:8)

The book of Acts begins with a post-resurrection interaction between Jesus and his disciples. Jesus teaches his disciples about "the kingdom of God" (Acts 1:3). They respond with a question about establishing a sociopolitical kingdom: "Lord, is this the time when you will restore the kingdom to Israel?" (Acts 1:6).[1] Jesus' response relates closely to our lives as workers.

> "It is not for you to know the times or periods that the Father has set by his own authority. But you will receive power when the Holy Spirit has come upon you; and you will be my witnesses in Jerusalem, in all Judea and Samaria, and to the ends of the earth." (Acts 1:7–8)

First, Jesus closes down the disciples' curiosity about the timeline of God's plan. "It is not for you to know the times or periods that the Father has set by his own authority" (Acts 1:7). We are to live in anticipation of the fullness of God's kingdom, but not in a way that wonders about the precise timing of God's return in Christ. Second, Jesus does not deny that God will establish a sociopolitical kingdom, that is, "restore the kingdom to Israel," as the disciples' question put it.

Jesus' disciples were all well versed in the Scriptures of Israel. They knew that the kingdom described by the prophets was no other-worldly reality, but that it was a real kingdom of peace and justice in a world renewed by the power of God. Jesus does not deny the reality of this coming kingdom, but he expands the boundaries of the disciples' expectation by including all creation in the hoped-for kingdom. This is not merely a new kingdom for the territory of Israel, but "in Jerusalem, and in all Judea and Samaria, and to the ends of the earth" (Acts 1:8). The fulfillment of this kingdom is not yet ("at this time") but it is here, in this world.

---

[1] *Apokathistēmi,* the restoration verb used by Luke, is used by the Septuagint and Josephus to describe Israel's hope for national restoration (see Exod. 4:7; Hos. 11:11; Josephus, *Antiquities of the Jews* 11.2, 14, *inter alia*). See also David L. Tiede, "The Exaltation of Jesus and the Restoration of Israel in Acts 1," *Harvard Theological Review* 79, no. 1 (1986): 278–86; and James D. G. Dunn, *Acts of the Apostles*, Epworth Commentaries (Peterborough, UK: Epworth Press, 1996), 4.

I saw the holy city, the new Jerusalem, coming down out of heaven from
God. . . . And I heard a loud voice from the throne saying, "See, the home
of God is among mortals." (Rev. 21:2–3)

The kingdom of heaven comes to earth, and God dwells here, in the
redeemed world. Why is it not here yet? Jesus' teaching suggests that
part of the answer is because his disciples have work to do. Human work
was needed to complete God's creation even in the Garden of Eden (Gen.
2:5), but our work was crippled by the Fall. In Acts 1 and 2, God sends
his Spirit to empower human work: "You will receive power when the
Holy Spirit has come upon you; and you will be my witnesses" (Acts
1:8a). Jesus is giving his followers a vocation—witnessing, in the sense
of bearing witness to the Spirit's power in every sphere of human activity—that is essential to the coming of the kingdom. God's gift of the Holy
Spirit fills the gap between the essential role that God assigned to human
work and our ability to fulfill that role. For the first time since the Fall,
our work has the power to contribute to fulfilling God's kingdom at the
return of Christ. Scholars, by and large, view Acts 1:8 as the program-
matic statement for this second of Luke's two volumes.

Indeed, the entire book of Acts can be taken as a (sometimes falter-
ing) expression of the Christian vocation to bear witness to the risen
Jesus. But bearing witness means far more than evangelizing. We must
not fall into the mistake of thinking Jesus is talking only about the work
of the individual sharing the gospel with an unbeliever through his or her
words. Instead, bearing witness to the coming kingdom primarily means
living now according to the principles and practices of God's kingdom.
We will come to see that the most effective form of Christian witness is
often—even primarily—the shared life of the community as it goes about
its work.

The shared Christian vocation of witness is possible only through
the power of the Holy Spirit. The Spirit transforms individuals and
communities in ways that result in the sharing of the fruits of human
labor—especially power, resources, and influence—with the community
and the surrounding culture. The community witnesses when the strong
aid the weak. The community witnesses when its members use their
resources to benefit the wider culture. The community witnesses when

those around them see that working in the ways of justice, goodness, and beauty leads to fuller life.

The locations mentioned by Jesus reveal that the witness of the disciples puts them in social danger. Jesus' group of Jewish disciples is commanded to speak for a man who has only recently been crucified as an enemy of the Roman Empire and a blasphemer of the God of Israel. They are called to take up this vocation in the city in which their teacher was killed, among the Samaritans—historic, ethnic enemies of the Jews— and in the broad reaches of the Roman Empire.[2]

In summary, Acts begins with an orienting vocation that calls Jesus' followers to the primary task of witness. Witness means, above all, living in accordance with the ways of God's coming kingdom. As we will see momentarily, the most important element of this life is that we work primarily for the good of others. This vocation is made possible by the power of the Holy Spirit and is to be exercised with little regard for social barriers. This orienting vocation does not denigrate the value of human work or the working lives of Jesus' disciples in favor of proclaiming Jesus by word alone—quite the opposite. Acts will argue forcefully that all human work can be a fundamental expression of God's kingdom.

An Orienting Identity as God's Kingdom Witnesses in Daily Life (Acts 2:1–41)

There is no question that the story of Pentecost is central to the life of the early Christian community. This is the event that initiates the vocation of witness described in Acts 1:8. This section of Acts makes claims on all workers in two ways. First, the Pentecost account identifies its Christian hearers within a new community that brings to life the re-creation of the world—that is, the kingdom of God—promised by God through the prophets. Peter explains the phenomenon at Pentecost by referring to the prophet Joel.

---

[2] For references to antipathy between Samaritans and Jews, see Josephus, *Antiquities of the Jews* 18:30; *Jewish War* 2:32ff. For the reference to the "ends of the earth" implying the full extent of peoples and places in the Roman Empire, see David W. Pao, *Acts and the Isaianic New Exodus* (Grand Rapids: Baker Academic, 2002), 91–96.

"These [men] are not drunk, as you suppose, for it is only nine o'clock
in the morning. No, this is what was spoken through the prophet Joel:
'In the last days it will be, God declares, that I will pour out my Spirit
upon all flesh, and your sons and your daughters shall prophesy, and
your young men shall see visions, and your old men shall dream dreams.
Even upon my slaves, both men and women, in those days I will pour
out my Spirit; and they shall prophesy. And I will show portents in the
heaven above and signs on the earth below, blood, and fire, and smoky
mist. The sun shall be turned to darkness and the moon to blood, before
the coming of the Lord's great and glorious day. Then everyone who
calls on the name of the Lord shall be saved.'" (Acts 2:15–21)

Peter refers to a section of Joel that describes the restoration of God's
exiled people. Peter uses this section to claim that God has initiated his
once-and-for-all deliverance of his people.[3] In the book of Joel, the return of God's people to the land both fulfills God's covenantal promises
and initiates the re-creation of the world. Joel describes this re-creation
with breathtaking imagery. As God's people return to the land, the desert
comes to life as a sort of new Eden. Dirt, animals, and people all rejoice
at the victory of God and the deliverance of God's people (see Joel 2).
Among the rich images in this section of Joel, we hear that the restoration of God's people will lead to immediate economic impact: "The LORD
said: 'I am sending you grain, wine, and oil, and you will be satisfied; and
I will no more make you a mockery among the nations'" (Joel 2:19). The
climax of this act of deliverance for Joel is the outpouring of the Spirit
upon the people of God. Peter understands the coming of the Spirit to
mean that the early Jesus-followers are—in some real, even if profoundly
mysterious, manner—participants in God's new world.

A second important and closely related point is that Peter describes
salvation as rescue from a "corrupt generation" (Acts 2:40). Two things
need clarification. First, Luke does not describe salvation as escape from

---

[3] The Christian modification of Israelite expectations about the end of the
age is called "inaugurated eschatology" and is often organized under the rubric
of a kingdom that is simultaneously *already* present and *not yet* consummated.
Israel expected the day of the Lord to come in one climactic stage. Early Christians
discovered that the day of the Lord was initiated at Jesus' resurrection and with
the outpouring of the Spirit, but that the kingdom would not come in full until
the return of Jesus.

this world into a heavenly existence. Instead, salvation begins right in the midst of this present world. Second, Luke expects that salvation has a present-tense component. It begins now as a different way of living, contrary to the patterns of this "corrupt generation." Because work and its economic and social consequences are so central to human identity, it should come as no surprise that one of the first patterns of human life to be reconstituted is the manner in which Christians manage their power and possessions. The flow, then, of this early section of Acts moves like this: (1) Jesus suggests that all human life should bear witness to Christ; (2) the coming of the Spirit marks the initiation of the long-promised "day of the Lord" and initiates people into God's new world; and (3) expectations of the "day of the Lord" include profound economic trans-formations. Luke's next move is to point to a new people, empowered by the Spirit, living according to a kingdom economy.

An Orienting Community That Practices the Ways of God's Kingdom (Acts 2:42–47; 4:32–37)

After Peter announces the Spirit's creation of a new kind of com-munity, Acts traces the rapid growth of such communities in a variety of places. The community summaries in Acts 2:42–47 and 4:32–37 are the most concentrated descriptions. Indeed, the texts themselves are remarkable in describing the scope of commitment and shared life of the early believers.[4] Because the summaries have many similarities, we will discuss them in tandem.

---

[4] Much has been written about the parallels between the community summa-ries and groups within Luke's historical context. Essene/Qumran parallels: Brian J. Capper, "The Interpretation of Acts 5.4," *Journal for the Study of the New Testament* 6, no. 19 (1983): 117–31; Brian J. Capper, "The Palestinian Cultural Context of Earliest Christian Community of Goods," in *The Book of Acts in Its Palestinian Setting*, ed. Richard J. Bauckham (Grand Rapids: Eerdmans, 1995), 323–56; Greco-Roman friendship parallels: Alan C. Mitchell, "The Social Func-tion of Friendship in Acts 2.44–47 and 4.32–37," *Journal of Biblical Literature* 111, no. 2 (1992): 255–72; Greco-Roman utopian parallels: Gregory E. Sterling, "'Athletes of Virtue': An Analysis of the Summaries in Acts (2.41–47; 4.32–35; 5.12–16)," *Journal of Biblical Literature* 113, no. 4 (1994): 679–96; parallels with Greco-Roman associations: Philip A. Harland, *Associations, Synagogues, and Congregations: Creating a Place in Ancient Mediterranean Society* (Min-

Acts 2:42–47 *They devoted themselves to the apostles' teaching and fellowship, to the breaking of bread and the prayers. Awe came upon everyone, because many wonders and signs were being done by the apostles. All who believed were together and had all things in common; they would sell their possessions and goods and distribute the proceeds to all, as any had need. Day by day, as they spent much time together in the temple, they broke bread at home and ate their food with glad and generous hearts, praising God and having the goodwill of all the people. And day by day the Lord added to their number those who were being saved.*

Acts 4:32–37 *Now the whole group of those who believed were of one heart and soul, and no one claimed private ownership of any possessions, but everything they owned was held in common. With great power the apostles gave their testimony to the resurrection of the Lord Jesus, and great grace was upon them all. There was not a needy person among them, for as many as owned lands or houses sold them and brought the proceeds of what was sold. They laid it at the apostles' feet, and it was distributed to each as any had need. There was a Levite, a native of Cyprus, Joseph, to whom the apostles gave the name Barnabas (which means "son of encouragement"). He sold a field that belonged to him, then brought the money, and laid it at the apostles' feet.*

While these texts do not describe work directly, they are keenly concerned with the deployment of power and possessions, two realities that are often an outcome of human labor. The first thing to note, in contrast to the surrounding society, is that Christian communities cultivate a very different set of practices with regard to the use of power and possessions. It is clear that the early Christians understood that the power and possessions of the individual were not to be saved for the comfort of the individual, but were to be expended or wisely invested for the good of the Christian community. Stated succinctly, goods are for the good of another. More than anything else, life in the kingdom of God means working for the good of others.

Two things should be stated here. First, these texts ask us to understand our identity primarily as members of the Christian community.

neapolis: Augsburg Fortress, 2003); John S. Kloppenborg, "Collegia and *Thiasoi*: Issues in Function, Taxonomy and Membership," in *Voluntary Associations in the Graeco-Roman World*, ed. John S. Kloppenborg and S. G. Wilson (London: Routledge, 1996), 16–30.

The good of the community is the good of each individual member. Second, this is a radical departure from the patronage economy that marked the Roman Empire. In a patronage system, gifts from the rich to the poor create a structure of systematic obligation. Every gift from a benefactor implies a social debt now owed by the beneficiary. This system created a sort of pseudo-generosity in which generous patrons often gave out of self-interest, seeking to accrue honor connected to patronage.[5] In essence, the Roman economy viewed "generosity" as a means to social power and status. These notions of systematic reciprocal obligation are completely absent in the descriptions in Acts 2 and 4. In the Christian community, giving is to be motivated by a genuine concern for the flourishing of the beneficiary, not for the honor of the benefactor. Giving has little to do with the giver and everything to do with the receiver.

This is a completely different socioeconomic system. Like Luke's Gospel, Acts regularly demonstrates that Christian conversion results in a reoriented approach to possessions and power. Moreover, this insistence that goods are to be used for the sake of the neighbor is patterned explicitly on Jesus' life, mission, and—primarily—his self-giving death.

The Economics of Radical Generosity (Acts 2:45; 4:34–35)

There is continuing debate about whether or not these community summaries advocate a certain economic system, with some commentators describing the practice of the community as "proto-communism" and others seeing a mandatory divestiture of goods. The text, however, does not suggest an attempt to change the structures beyond the Christian community. Indeed, it would be difficult to think of a small, marginalized, socially powerless group having designs on changing the imperial economic system. It is clear that the community did not fully opt out of the economic systems of the empire. Likely, fishermen remained members of fishing cartels and artisans continued to do business in the market.[6] Paul, after all, continued making tents to support his missionary travels (Acts 18:3).

---

[5] It is not difficult to notice that giving within the Christian community can still function in this way.

[6] See Harland; also Kloppenborg.

Rather, the text suggests something far more demanding. In the earliest church, people of means and power liquidated their goods for the sake of the less powerful "from time to time" (Acts 4:34, NIV) as anyone "had need" (Acts 2:45; 4:35). This describes a kind of radical availability as the normal status of each person's possessions. That is, the resources—material, political, social, or practical—of any member were put at the constant disposal of the Christian community, even while individual members continued to oversee their particular resources. Rather than systematically prescribing the distribution of wealth in such a way as to ensure flat equality, the earliest church accepted the reality of economic disequalibrium, but practiced a radical generosity whereby goods properly existed for the benefit of the whole, not the individual. This form of generosity is, in many ways, more challenging than a rigid system of rules. It calls for ongoing responsiveness, mutual involvement in the lives of community members, and a continual willingness to hold possessions loosely, valuing the relationships within the community more than the (false) security of possessions.[7]

It is highly likely that this system within a system was inspired by the economic ideals expressed in Israel's law, climaxing with the practice of Jubilee—the once-in-fifty-years redistribution of land and wealth within Israel (Lev. 25:1–55). Jubilee was designed by God to ensure that all people had access to the means of making a living, an ideal that appears never to have been widely practiced by God's people. Jesus, however, introduces his ministry with a set of texts from Isaiah 61 and 58 that produce a great many Jubilee themes:

> "The Spirit of the Lord is upon me, because he has anointed me to bring good news to the poor. He has sent me to proclaim release to the captives and recovery of sight to the blind, to let the oppressed go free, to proclaim the year of the Lord's favor." (Luke 4:18–19)

Jubilee ethic is further alluded to in Acts 4:34, where Luke tells us that "there were no needy persons among them." This appears to be a

---

[7] Christopher M. Hays, *Luke's Wealth Ethics: A Study in Their Coherence and Character*, Wissenschaftliche Untersuchungen zum Neuen Testament 2.275 (Tubingen: Mohr-Siebeck, 2010), explores the ethics of wealth in Luke and Acts in depth.

direct echo of Deuteronomy 15:4, where the practice of the Sabbath year (a mini-Jubilee occurring once every seven years) is designed to ensure that "there will be no one in need among you."

It is fitting that the Christian community would see this as a model for their economic life. But whereas in ancient Israel the Sabbath year and the Jubilee were to be practiced only every seven and fifty years, respectively, radical availability marked the resources of the early Christian community. We can imagine it in terms similar to the Sermon on the Mount. "You have heard that it was said of old, 'Give back your land to those who are landless once every fifty years,' but I say to you, 'Make your power and resources available any time you see the need.'" Radical generosity based on the needs of others becomes the basis of economic practice in the Christian community. We will explore this in depth through the incidents in the book of Acts.

The practices of the early churches challenge contemporary Christians to think imaginatively about models for radical generosity today. How could radical availability stand as a witness to the kingdom of God and form a plausible alternative way of structuring human life in a culture marked by the tenacious pursuit of personal wealth and security?

The Holy Spirit Empowers Radical Generosity with Every Kind of Resource (Acts 2:42–47; 4:32–37)

Two final points are important to note with regard to the use of resources in the early Christian community. First is the necessity of the Holy Spirit to the practice of radical generosity. The descriptions of the community in Acts 2:42–47 and 4:32–37 follow immediately from the first two major manifestations of the Holy Spirit. Luke could not be clearer in forging a link between the Spirit's presence and power and the ability of the community to live with Christ-like generosity. We must understand that one of the fundamental works of the Spirit in the life of the early Christians was the cultivation of a community that took a radically different stance toward the deployment of resources. So, while we often get caught up in looking for the more spectacular manifestations of the Spirit (visions, tongues, and so on), we need to reckon with the fact that the simple act of sharing or consistent hospitality might be one of the most magnificent gifts of the Holy Spirit.

Second, lest we begin to think that this word is only for those with financial resources, we see Peter and John demonstrate that all resources are to be used for the sake of others. In Acts 3:1–10, Peter and John encounter a beggar at the gate of the temple. The beggar is looking for money, though Peter and John have none. They do, however, have a witness to the coming of the kingdom through the life, death, and resurrection of Jesus. Hence, Peter replies, "Silver or gold I do not have, but what I have I give you. In the name of Jesus Christ of Nazareth, walk" (Acts 3:6). Here is an example of resource-sharing that is not connected to monetary wealth. The use of power and position to build community will occur on several further occasions in Acts.

Perhaps the most moving expression occurs when Barnabas—who, in Acts 4:32–37, is an example of radical generosity of financial resources—also puts his social resources at Paul's disposal, helping welcome him into the reluctant fellowship of the apostles in Jerusalem (see Acts 9:26–27). Another example is Lydia, who employs her high social standing in the textile industry in Thyatira as a means of entry for Paul into the city (Acts 16:11–15). Social capital is to be deployed, like any other capital, for the good of the kingdom as understood by the Christian community.

A Just Community Is a Witness to the World (Acts 2:47; 6:7)

When resources are properly deployed in the life of the Christian community—as they are after the selection of the table servers in Acts 6—the community becomes a magnet. The community's life of justice—marked primarily by the other-centered use of power and possessions—draws people to it and to its head, Jesus. When the community uses its possessions and privileges to give life to those in need, when the resources of the individual are fully committed to benefit others in the community, people flock to join. We have seen already that "the Lord added to their number daily those who were being saved" (Acts 2:47). It is evident in the aftermath of the Spirit-empowered service in Acts 6 as well. The community-forming, justice-promoting work of the seven deacons results in life for many: "The word of God continued to spread; the number of the disciples increased greatly in Jerusalem, and a great many of the priests became obedient to the faith" (Acts 6:7).

A Clash of Kingdoms: Community and Power (Acts 5–7)

Acts takes place in the earthy reality of a genuine community, and it does not gloss over the threat that the effects of sin pose to communities. The first two major threats to the Christian community that Luke presents are resource-related issues. As we will see, Ananias and Sapphira, as well as the Hebrew/Aramaic speaking sector of the community, fall into sin in relation to their stewardship of resources and power. For Luke, this defect threatens the very life of the community.

Ananias and Sapphira: A Case of Malicious Identity (Acts 5:1–11)

The deaths of Ananias and Sapphira (Acts 5:1–11) are nothing if not frightful and puzzling. The two, a married couple, sell a piece of property and publicly give the proceeds to the community. However, they secretly hold back a portion of the money for themselves. Peter detects the deception and confronts the two separately. Merely hearing Peter's accusation causes each of them to fall dead on the spot. To our ears, their fate seems out of proportion to their infraction. Peter acknowledges that they were under no obligation to donate the money. "While it remained unsold, did it not remain your own?" he says. "And after it was sold, were not the proceeds at your disposal?" (Acts 5:4). Private property has not been abolished, and even those in the community of love-for-neighbor may legitimately choose to hold the resources God has entrusted to them. So why does lying about the money bring instant death?

Many attempts have been made to describe the reason for their deaths and even simply to name the sin they committed.[8] It appears, fundamentally, that Ananias and Sapphira's transgression is that they are counterfeit community members. As the scholar Scott Bartchy puts it, "By lying in order to achieve an honor they had not earned, Ananias and Sapphira not only dishonored and shamed themselves as patrons

---

[8] See options for interpretation in Joseph A. Fitzmyer, *The Acts of the Apostles*, *The Anchor Bible* (New York: Doubleday, 1998), 318–19.

but also revealed themselves to be outsiders, non-kin."[9] They are not so much misers as imposters.[10]

Their deceit demonstrates that they are still functioning as members of the Roman patronage system, while they pretend to have become members of the Christian love-of-neighbor system. They attempt to look like Barnabas in his other-centered approach to stewarding resources (Acts 4:36–37). But their motivation is actually to gain honor for themselves on the cheap. In so doing, they actually function as part of the Roman patronage economy. They look generous, but they are giving for the sake of status, not love. Moreover, their lie about their stewardship of resources is interpreted by Peter as a lie to the Holy Spirit and to God (Acts 5:3–4). How striking that a lie to the community is equated with a lie to the Spirit of God! And a lie about resources is as serious as a lie about "religious" matters. We have seen already that one of the primary roles of the Holy Spirit is to form God's people into a community that uses resources in accordance with a deep concern for others. It is not surprising, then, that Ananias and Sapphira's faked act of generosity is depicted as falsifying the work of the Spirit. Their false generosity and their attempt to deceive the Holy Spirit are a threat to the identity of the Christian community. This is a sober reminder of the serious stakes connected to the Christian community and to our own participation within it.

Ananias and Sapphira's deceit occurs in the realm of money. What if it occurred in the realm of work itself? What if they had falsely pretended to serve their masters as though serving God (Col. 3:22–24), or to treat subordinates justly (Col. 3:25), or to engage in conflict honestly (Matt. 18:15–17)? Would deceiving the Christian community about such things have caused a similarly unacceptable threat to the community?

---

[9] S. Scott Bartchy, "Community of Goods in Acts: Idealization or Social Reality?" in *The Future of Early Christianity: Essays in Honor of Helmut Koester*, ed. Birger A. Pearson, A. Thomas Krabel, George W. E. Nickelsburg, and Norman R. Petersen (Minneapolis: Fortress Press, 1991), 316.

[10] For a full treatment of this narrative with respect to economic and communal implications, see Aaron J. Kuecker, "The Spirit and the 'Other,' Satan and the 'Self': Economic Ethics as a Consequence of Identity Transformation in Luke-Acts," in *Engaging Economics: New Testament Scenarios and Early Christian Reception,* ed. Bruce W. Longenecker and Kelly D. Liebengood (Grand Rapids: Eerdmans, 2009), 81–103.

Luke doesn't report any such cases in Acts, yet the same principle applies. Genuinely belonging to the Christian community carries with it a fundamental change in our orientation. We now act in all ways—including work—to love our neighbors as ourselves, not to increase our social status, wealth, and power.

The Spirit and the Worker (Acts 6:1–7)

Themes from the account of Ananias and Sapphira are present in Acts 6:1–7, which marks the first intra-group dispute in the Christian community. The Hellenists are probably Greek-speaking Jews who have returned to Jerusalem from one of the many Diaspora communities in the Roman Empire. The Hebrews are probably Jews who are from the historic land of Israel (Palestine) and who primarily speak Aramaic and/ or Hebrew. It takes very little social imagination to see what is happening in this situation. In a community that sees itself as the fulfillment of Israel's covenant with God, members who are more prototypically Israelite are receiving more of the group's resources than the others. This sort of situation happens regularly in our world. Those who are most similar to the leaders of a movement on the basis of background, culture, status, and so on often benefit from their identity in ways unavailable to those who are in some way different.

Serving the Word and Serving Tables Are Equally Valuable (Acts 6:2–4)

One of the greatest contributions that Acts makes to a theology of work emerges from the apostles' response to the intra-community injustice of Acts 6:1–7. The work of administering justice—in this case, by overseeing food distribution—is just as important as the work of preaching the word. This may not be clear at first because of a misleading translation in the NRSV and the NIV:

> The twelve called together the whole community of the disciples and said, "It is not right that we should neglect the word of God in order to wait on tables." (Acts 6:2, NRSV)

> "It would not be right for us to neglect the ministry of the word of God in order to wait on tables." (Acts 6:2, NIV)

It is hard not to read some condescension in the voices of the apostles in these English translations. In the minds of some, working with the word of God is "ministry" (as the NIV puts it), while the work of "waiting" at tables is somehow menial. One line of interpretation has followed this sense, suggesting that waiting on tables was "trivial,"[11] a "humble task"[12] or one of the "lower tasks"[13] in the community. This line of interpretation sees Stephen's subsequent preaching as the "real" purpose behind the Spirit's influence in 6:3.[14] There would be no need for the Holy Spirit to get involved in the menial task of managing the allocation of resources.

But this line of argument depends on dubious translations. The Greek verb translated as "wait" in the NRSV and NIV is *diakoneō*, which carries the sense of service or ministry. The King James Version and the NASB put it more accurately as "serve."

> "It is not reason [i.e., right] that we should leave the word of God, and serve tables." (Acts 6:2, KJV)

> "It is not desirable for us to neglect the word of God in order to serve tables." (Acts 6:2, NASB)

Moreover, just a few words later, in Acts 6:3–4, even the NRSV and the NIV translate the same word as "serving" and "ministry," respectively.

> "We, for our part, will devote ourselves to prayer and to serving the word." (Acts 6:3–4, NRSV)

> "[We] will give our attention to prayer and the ministry of the word." (Acts 6:4, NIV)

In other words, the Greek word for the work of the word is exactly the same (in verb form) as the word for the work of distributing resources,

---

[11] Fitzmyer, 344.

[12] John Michael Penney, "The Missionary Emphasis of Lukan Pneumatology," *Journal of Pentecostal Theology* (Sheffield, UK: Sheffield Academic Press, 1997), 65n11.

[13] Joseph T. Lienhard, "Acts 6.1–6: A Redactional View," *Catholic Biblical Quarterly* 37 (1975): 232.

[14] Youngmo Cho, *Spirit and Kingdom in the Writings of Luke and Paul* (Waynesborough, GA; Paternoster, 2005), 132.

diakonia, "serving." The NRSV and NIV translators rightly regard the work of preaching as "serving" and "ministry." Yet they condescend to a more demeaning word when referring to the work of food distribution, "waiting" tables. In contrast, the KJV and NASB translators do not read such condescension into the text. Whether working with the word or with food on tables, both groups "serve" in these translations.

The Greek text gives the important sense that the work of serving those in need is on par with the apostolic work of prayer and preaching. The apostles serve the word, and the deacons (as they have come to be called) serve those in need. Their service is qualitatively the same, although the specific tasks and skills are different. Both are essential in the formation of God's people and for the witness of God's people in the world. The life of the community depends upon these forms of service, and Luke does not give us the sense that one is more powerful or more spiritual than the other.

Despite all this, could it be argued that the condescension is not just a matter of translation but is really present in the disciples' own words? Could the apostles themselves have imagined that they were chosen to serve the word because they were more gifted than those who were chosen to serve tables? If so, they would be falling back into something similar to the Roman patronage system, setting themselves up with a status too high to sully by serving tables. They would be substituting a new source of status (gifts of the Holy Spirit) for the old Roman one (patronage). The gospel of Christ goes deeper than this! In the Christian community there is no source of status.

Ironically, one of the table-servers, Stephen, turns out to be even more gifted as a preacher than most of the apostles (Acts 6:8–7:60). Yet despite his preaching gift, he is set aside for the service of resource distribution. At that moment, at least, it was more important to God's purposes for him to work as a table-server than as a word-server. For him, at least, no lingering hunger for status stands in the way of accepting this call to serve tables.

The Work of Community Leadership Is a Work of the Holy Spirit (Acts 6:3)

The workers best suited to heal the ethnic divide in the Acts 6 community are qualified because they are known to be "full of the Spirit and of wisdom." Like those qualified for prayer and preaching, the table-servers' ability is the result of spiritual power. Nothing less than the power of the Spirit makes possible meaningful, community-building, peace-making work among Christians. This passage helps us to see that all work that builds the community or, more broadly, that promotes justice, goodness, and beauty, is—in a deep sense—service (or ministry) to the world.

In our churches, do we recognize the equal ministry of the pastor who preaches the word, the mother and father who provide a loving home for their children, and the accountant who gives a just and honest statement of her employer's expenditures? Do we understand that they are all reliant upon the Spirit to do their work for the good of the community? Every manner of good work has the capacity—by the power of the Spirit—to be a means of participation in God's renewal of the world.

Work and Identity (Acts 8–12)

The next section of Acts moves the Christian community, by the power of the Spirit, across cultural barriers as the gospel of Jesus Christ is extended to foreigners (Samaritans), social outcasts (the Ethiopian eunuch), enemies (Saul), and all ethnicities (Gentiles). This section tends to introduce figures by giving their occupation (roughly rendered). In this section we meet:

- Simon, a sorcerer (Acts 8:9–24)

- An Ethiopian eunuch, who is an important economic official for the queen of Ethiopia (Acts 8:27)

- Saul, the Pharisee and persecutor of Christians (Acts 9:1)

- Tabitha, a garment maker (Acts 9:36–43)

- Cornelius, a Roman centurion (Acts 10:1)

- Simon, a tanner (Acts 10:5)

- Herod, a king (Acts 12)

Issues of work are not Luke's main concern in this section, so we must be careful not to make too much of the naming of occupations. Luke's point is that the way these people exercise their vocation marks them as heading either toward the kingdom or away from it.

Those headed into the kingdom use the fruits of their labor to serve others as witnesses of God's kingdom. Those headed away from the kingdom use the fruits of their labor solely for personal gain. This is evident from a short summary of some of these characters. Several of them seek only personal gain from their work and its accompanying power and resources:

- Simon offers money to the apostles so that he can have power to bestow the Holy Spirit (Acts 8:18–19)—a clear effort to maintain his social status as a "man [who] is the power of God that is called Great" (Acts 8:10).

- Saul uses his network of relationships to persecute followers of Jesus (Acts 9:1–2), in order to protect the social status he enjoyed as a zealous Jew (Acts 22:3) and Pharisee (Acts 26:5).

- Herod uses his power as Rome's client-king to bolster his popularity by killing James the apostle (Acts 12:1–2). Herod later allows himself to be acclaimed as a god, the ultimate patronage status claimed by the Roman emperors (Acts 12:20–23).

The consequences of these acts are dire. Simon is strongly rebuked by Peter (Acts 8:20–23). Saul is confronted by the risen Jesus, who identifies himself with the very community Paul is persecuting (Acts 9:3–9). Herod is struck dead by an angel of the Lord and eaten by worms (Acts 12:23). Standing in counterpoint to them are several people who use their position, power, or resources to bless and bring life:

- Tabitha, a garment-maker, makes clothes to share with widows in her community (Acts 9:39).

- Simon, a leather-worker, opens his home to Peter (Acts 10:5).

- Cornelius, a Roman centurion already known for generosity (Acts 10:4), uses his connections to invite a great number of friends and family to hear the preaching of Peter (Acts 10:24).

Though he was introduced prior to this section, Barnabas—who we know from Acts 4:37 is a Levite—uses his position within the community to graft Saul into the apostolic fellowship, even when the apostles resist (Acts 9:26–27), and to validate the conversions of Gentiles in Antioch (Acts 11:22–24). We should note that Acts 11:24 shares the secret of Barnabas's ability to use his resources and position in such a way as to build the community of Christians. There we learn explicitly that Barnabas was "full of the Holy Spirit."

The message in all these examples is consistent. The power, prestige, position, and resources that arise from work are meant to be used for the sake of others—and not only for one's own benefit. This, again, is modeled on no less a figure than Jesus, who in Luke's Gospel uses his authority for the benefit of the world and not only for his own sake.

Acts 11:27–30 gives a community example of the use of resources for the good of others in need. In response to a Spirit-inspired prophecy of a worldwide famine, "The disciples determined that according to their ability, each would send relief to the believers living in Judea" (Acts 11:29). Here we see the use of the fruit of human labor for the benefit of others. And here we see that this sort of generosity was not merely spontaneous and episodic but planned, organized, and deeply intentional. (The collection for the church in Jerusalem is discussed further in the section on 1 Corinthians 16:1–3 in "1 Corinthians and Work.")

Acts 11:1–26 begins an account of how the Christian community resolved a deep dispute about whether a Gentile must convert to Judaism before becoming a follower of Jesus. This dispute is discussed in an article on chapter 15 below.

A Clash of Kingdoms: Community and Power Brokers (Acts 13–19)

We will explore this section according to four main themes relevant to the theology of work that emerges from Acts. First, we will examine one further passage relating to vocation as witness. Second, we will discuss how the Christian community exercises the power of leadership and decision-making itself. Third, we will look at how the Spirit-led community engages the powers that be in the wider culture. Fourth, we will examine whether following Christ rules out certain forms of vocation and civic engagement. Finally, we will explore Paul's own practice of continuing to work as a tentmaker on his missionary journeys.

Vocation in the Context of Community (Acts 13:1–3)

Acts 13:1–3 introduces us to a set of practices in the church at Antioch. This community is remarkable both for its ethnic diversity and its commitment to practical witness of the kingdom of God.[15] We have seen already how Luke shows that work—especially the use of power and resources—functions as a form of witness.[16] We have seen in Acts 6:1–7 that this applies equally to vocations we naturally associate with ministry (such as being a missionary) and those we are more likely to call "work" (such as hospitality). All vocations have the potential to serve and witness the kingdom, especially when employed in the pursuit of justice and righteousness.

Acts 13:1–3 shows the Christian community trying to discern how the Spirit is leading them to witness. Paul and Barnabas are singled out to work as traveling evangelists and healers. What is remarkable is that this discernment is accomplished communally. The Christian community, rather than the individual, is best able to discern the vocations of its individual members. This could mean that today's Christian communities should participate alongside families and young people as they seek answers for questions such as, "What do you want to do when you grow up?" "What will you do after graduation?" or "To what is God calling you?" This would require Christian communities to develop a much greater expertise in vocational discernment than is presently common. It would also require them to take a much more serious interest in work that serves the world beyond the structures of the church. Merely asserting authority over young people's work lives is not enough. Young people

---

[15] Ben Witherington III, *The Acts of the Apostles: A Socio-Rhetorical Commentary* (Grand Rapids: Eerdmans, 1998), 392.

[16] It is worth noting, once again, that the proper function of the community—marked particularly by generosity, economic justice, and God-and-other-centered love—regularly results in the growth of the kingdom (Acts 2:47; 6:7; 9:31; etc.).

will pay attention only if the Christian community can help them do a fuller job of discernment than they can do by other means.

Doing this well would be a double form of witness. First, young people from all religious traditions—and those who have no tradition—struggle deeply with the burden of choosing or finding work. Imagine if the Christian community could genuinely help reduce their burden and improve the outcomes. Second, the great majority of Christians work outside the structures of the church. Imagine if all of us engaged in our work as a means of Christian service to the world, improving the lives of the billions of people we work alongside and on behalf of. How much more visible would that make Christ in the world?

Community discernment of vocation continues throughout Acts, with Paul taking many missionary partners from the community—Barnabas, Timothy, Silas, and Priscilla, to name but a few. Second, testifying again to Luke's realism, we see that this shared vocation to witness does not eliminate the relational tension brought about by human sinfulness. Paul and Barnabas have such a serious dispute over the inclusion of John Mark (who had deserted the team on a previous engagement) that they go their separate ways (Acts 15:36–40).

Leadership and Decision-Making in the Christian Community (Acts 15)

An example of the radical reorienting of social interactions in the Christian community arises during a deep dispute about whether Gentile Christians must adopt Jewish laws and customs. In hierarchical Roman society, the patron of a social organization would dictate such a decision to his followers, perhaps after listening to various opinions. But in the Christian community, important decisions are made by the group as whole, relying on their equal access to the guidance of the Holy Spirit.

The dispute actually begins in chapter 11. Peter experiences a surprising revelation that God is offering "the repentance that leads to life" (Acts 11:18) to Gentiles without requiring them to become Jews first. But when he travels to Jerusalem in the company of some uncircumcised (Gentile) men, some of the Christians there complain that he is violating Jewish law (Acts 11:1–2). When challenged in this way, Peter does not become angry, does not attempt to lord it over the men by reminding them of his leading position among Jesus' disciples, does not denigrate their opinions, and does not impugn their motives. Instead, he tells the story of what happened to lead him to this conclusion and how he sees God's hand in it: "If then God gave them the same gift that he gave us when we believed in the Lord Jesus Christ, who was I that I could hinder God?" (Acts 11:17). Notice that he portrays himself not as wise, nor morally superior, but as one who was on the verge of making a serious mistake until corrected by God.

Then he leaves it to his challengers to respond. Having heard Peter's experience, they do not react defensively, do not challenge Peter's authority in the name of James (the Lord's brother and the leader of the Jerusalem church), and do not accuse Peter of exceeding his authority. Instead, they too look for God's hand at work and reach the same conclusion as Peter. What began as a confrontation ends with fellowship and praise. "When they heard this, they were silenced. And they praised God" (Acts 11:18). We can't expect every dispute to be resolved so amicably, but we can see that when people acknowledge and explore the grace of God in one another's lives, there is every reason to hope for a mutually upbuilding outcome.

Peter departs Jerusalem in concord with his former antagonists, but there remain others in Judea who are teaching that Gentiles must first convert to Judaism. "Unless you are circumcised according to the custom of Moses," they say, "you cannot be saved" (Acts 15:1). Paul and Barnabas are in Antioch at the time, and they, like Peter, have experienced God's grace to the Gentiles without any need for conversion to Judaism. The text tells us that the division was serious, but a mutual decision was made to seek the wisdom of the Christian community as a whole. "After Paul and Barnabas had no small dissension and debate with them, Paul and Barnabas and some of the others were appointed to go up to Jerusalem to discuss this question with the apostles and the elders" (Acts 15:2).

They arrive in Jerusalem and are greeted warmly by the apostles and elders (Acts 15:4). Those who hold the opposite opinion—that Gentiles must first convert to Judaism—are also present (Acts 15:5). They all decide to meet to consider the matter and engage in a lively debate

(Acts 15:6). Then Peter, who is of course among the apostles in Jerusalem, repeats the story of how God revealed to him his grace for the Gentiles without the need to convert to Judaism (Acts 15:7). Paul and Barnabas report their similar experiences, also focusing on what God is doing rather than claiming any superior wisdom or authority (Acts 15:12). All the speakers receive a respectful hearing. Then the group considers what each has said in the light of Scripture (Acts 15:15–17). James, functioning as the head of the church in Jerusalem, proposes a resolution. "I have reached the decision that we should not trouble those Gentiles who are turning to God, but we should write to them to abstain only from things polluted by idols and from fornication and from whatever has been strangled and from blood" (Acts 15:19–20).

If James were exercising authority like a Roman patron, that would be the end of the matter. His status alone would decide the issue. But this is not how the decision unfolds in the Christian community. The community does accept his decision, but as a matter of agreement, not command. Not only James, but all the leaders—in fact, the entire church—have a say in the decision. "The apostles and the elders, with the consent of the whole church, decided . . ." (Acts 15:22). And when they send word to the Gentile churches of their decision "to impose on you no further burden" (Acts 15:28b), they do so in the name of the whole body, not the name of James as patron. "We have decided unanimously to choose representatives and send them to you" (Acts 15:25). Moreover, they claim no personal authority, but only that they have tried to be obedient to the Holy Spirit. "For it has seemed good to the Holy Spirit and to us . . . ," they report (Acts 15:28a). The word *seem* indicates a humility about their decision, underscoring that they have renounced the Roman patronage system with its claims of power, prestige, and status.

Before we leave this episode, let us notice one more element of it. The leaders in Jerusalem show remarkable deference to the experience of workers in the field—Peter, Paul, and Barnabas—working on their own far from headquarters, each facing a particular situation that required a practical decision. The leaders in Jerusalem highly respect their experience and judgment. They communicate carefully about the principles that should guide decisions (Acts 15:19–21), but they delegate decision-making to those closest to the action, and they confirm the decisions made by Peter, Paul, and Barnabas in the field. Again, this is a radical departure from the Roman patronage system, which concentrated power and authority in the hands of the patron.

The beneficial effects of the practice of uniform education about mission, principles, and values combined with localized delegation of decision-making and action are well known because of their widespread adoption by business, military, educational, nonprofit, and government institutions in the second half of the twentieth century. The management of virtually every type of organization has been radically transformed by it. The resulting unleashing of human creativity, productivity, and service would be no surprise to the leaders of the early church, who experienced the same explosion in the rapid expansion of the church in the apostolic age.

However, it is not clear that churches today have fully adopted this lesson with respect to economic activity. For example, Christians work-ing in developing countries often complain that they are hampered by the rigid stances of churches far away in the developed world. Well-meaning boycotts, fair-trade rules, and other pressure tactics may have the opposite consequences of what was intended. For example, an eco-nomic development missionary in Bangladesh reported about negative results of the imposition of child labor restrictions by his sponsoring organization in the United States. A company he was helping develop was required to stop buying materials that were produced using workers under sixteen years old. One of their suppliers was a company consisting of two teenaged brothers. Because of the new restrictions, the company had to stop buying parts from the brothers, which left their family with-out any source of income. So their mother had to return to prostitution, which made things much worse for the mother, the brothers, and the rest of the family. "What we need from the church in the U.S. is fellowship that is not oppressive," the missionary later said. "Having to comply with well-intentioned Western Christian dictates means we have to hurt people in our country."[17]

---

[17] Name of source withheld at his request due to security concerns. Notes taken by William Messenger at the Theology of Work Project Conference, Hong Kong, July 29, 2010.

The Community of the Spirit Confronts the Brokers of Power (Acts 16; 19)

In the latter half of Acts, Paul, his companions, and various Christian communities come into conflict with those who wield local economic and civic power. The first incident occurs in Pisidian Antioch, where "the devout women of high standing and the leading men of the city" (Acts 13:50) are incited against Paul and Barnabas and expel them from the city. Then, in Iconium, Paul and Barnabas are maltreated by "both Gentiles and Jews, with their rulers" (Acts 14:5). In Philippi, Paul and Silas are imprisoned for "disturbing" the city (Acts 16:19–24). Paul has run-ins with the city officials of Thessalonica (Acts 17:6–9) and the proconsul of Achaia (Acts 18:12). Later, he comes into conflict with the silversmiths' guild of Ephesus (Acts 19:23–41). The conflicts culminate with Paul's trial for disturbing the peace in Jerusalem, which occupies the final eight chapters of Acts.

These confrontations with local powers should not be surprising given the coming of God's Spirit announced by Peter in Acts 2. There we saw that the coming of the Spirit was—in some mysterious way—the initiation of God's new world. This was bound to threaten the powers of the old world. We have seen that the Spirit worked in the community to form a gift-based economy very different from the Roman economy based on patronage. Christian communities formed a system-within-a-system, where believers still participated in the Roman economy but had a different manner of using resources. Conflict with local leaders was precisely due to the fact that these leaders had the greatest stake in maintaining Rome's patronage economy.

The confrontations in Acts 16:16–24 and Acts 19:23–41 both merit deeper discussion. In them, the shape of the kingdom clashes deeply with economic practices of the Roman world.

Confrontation over the Liberation of a Slave Girl in Philippi (Acts 16:16–24)

The first of the two confrontations occurs in Philippi, where Paul and Silas encounter a girl with a spirit of divination.[18] In the Greco-Roman

---

[18] See John R. Levison, *Filled with the Spirit* (Grand Rapids: Eerdmans, 2009), 318–20, for a description of this type of spirit in Greco-Roman perceptions.

context, this type of spirit was associated with fortune-telling—a connection that "brought her owners a great deal of money" (Acts 16:16). This
seems to be an example of the grossest form of economic exploitation.
It is puzzling that Paul and Silas do not act more quickly (Acts 16:18).
Perhaps the reason is that Paul wants to make a connection with her or
her owners before correcting them. When Paul does act, however, the
result is spiritual liberation for the girl and financial loss for her owners.
The owners respond by dragging Paul and Silas before the authorities
on charges of disturbing the peace.

This incident demonstrates powerfully that the ministry of liberation Jesus proclaimed in Luke 4 can run counter to at least one
common business practice, the exploitation of slaves. Businesses that
produce economic profit at the expense of human exploitation are in
conflict with the Christian gospel. (Governments that exploit humans
are just as bad. We discussed earlier how Herod's violence against his
people and even his own soldiers led to his death at the hands of an
angel of the Lord). Paul and Silas were not on a mission to reform the
corrupt economic and political practices of the Roman world, but the
power of Jesus to liberate people from sin and death cannot help but
break the bonds of exploitation. There can be no spiritual liberation
without economic consequences. Paul and Silas were willing to expose
themselves to ridicule, beating, and prison in order to bring economic
liberation to someone whose sex, economic status, and age made her
vulnerable to abuse.

If we look ahead two thousand years, is it possible that Christians
have accommodated to, or even profited from, products, companies, industries, and governments that violate Christian ethical and social principles? It is easy to rail against illegal industries such as narcotics and
prostitution, but what about the many legal industries that harm workers, consumers, or the public at large? What about the legal loopholes,
subsidies, and unfair government regulations that benefit some citizens
at the expense of others? Do we even recognize how we may benefit
from the exploitation of others? In a global economy, it can be difficult
to trace the conditions and consequences of economic activity. Well-
informed discernment is needed, and the Christian community has not
always been rigorous in its critiques. In fact, the book of Acts does not

give principles for gauging economic activity. But it does demonstrate that economic matters are gospel matters. In the persons of Paul and Silas, two of the greatest missionaries and heroes of the faith, we have all the proof we need that Christians are called to confront the economic abuses of the world.

Chapters 17 and 18 contains much of interest with regard to work, but for the sake of continuing the discussion of confrontations arising from the gospel's challenge to the systems of the world, this article is followed by the account of the confrontation in Acts 19:21–41, returning then to chapters 17, 18, and the other parts of chapter 19.

Confrontation over the Disruption of Trade in Ephesus (Acts 19:21–41)

The following discussion falls a little out of order (skipping over Acts 19:17–20 for the moment) so that we can cover the second incident of confrontation. It occurs in Ephesus, home to the Temple of Artemis. The Artemis cult in Ephesus was a powerful economic force in Asia Minor. Pilgrims streamed to the temple (a structure so grand that it was considered one of the Seven Wonders of the Ancient World) in hopes of receiving from Artemis enhanced success in the hunt, in the field, or in the family. In this context, as with other tourism centers, many of the local industries were tied to the ongoing relevance of the attraction.[19]

A man named Demetrius, a silversmith who made silver shrines of Artemis, brought no little business to the artisans. These he gathered together, with the workers of the same trade, and said: "Men, you know that we get our wealth from this business. You also see and hear that not only in Ephesus but in almost the whole of Asia this Paul has persuaded and drawn away a considerable number of people by saying that gods made with hands are not gods. And there is danger not only that this trade of ours may come into disrepute but also that the temple of the great goddess Artemis will be scorned, and she will be deprived of her majesty that brought all Asia and the world to worship her." When they heard this, they were enraged and shouted: "Great is Artemis of the Ephesians!" The city was filled with the confusion; and people rushed together to the theater, dragging with them Gaius and Aristarchus, Macedonians who were Paul's travel companions. (Acts 19:24–29)

---

[19] See Witherington, 592–93.

As Demetrius recognizes, when people become followers of Jesus, they can be expected to change the way they use their money. Ceasing to buy items related to idol worship is merely the most obvious change. Christians might also be expected to spend less on luxury items for themselves and more on necessities for the benefit of others. Perhaps they will consume less and donate or invest more in general. There is nothing prohibiting Christians from buying silver items in general. But Demetrius is right to see that patterns of consumption will change if many people start believing in Jesus. This will always be threatening to those profiting most from the way things were before.

This prompts us to wonder which aspects of economic life in our own context might be incommensurate with the Christian gospel. For example, is it possible that, contrary to Demetrius's fears, Christians have continued to buy goods and services incompatible with following Jesus? Have we become Christians, yet continued to buy the equivalent of silver shrines to Artemis? Certain "aspirational" branded items come to mind, which appeal to buyers' desires to associate themselves with the social status, wealth, power, intelligence, beauty, or other attributes implied by the items' "brand promise." If Christians claim that their standing comes solely from the unconditional love of God in Christ, does self-association with brands function as a kind of idolatry? Is buying a prestigious brand essentially similar to buying a silver shrine to Artemis? This incident in Ephesus warns us that following Jesus has economic consequences that may make us uncomfortable at times, to say the least.

Engaging the Culture with Respect (Acts 17:16–34)

Despite the need to confront the power brokers in the wider culture, confrontation is not always the best way for the Christian community to engage the world. Often, the culture is misguided, struggling, or ignorant of God's grace, but not actually oppressive. In these cases, the best way to proclaim the gospel may be to cooperate with the culture and engage it with respect.

In Acts 17, Paul provides a model for engaging the culture respectfully. It begins with observation. Paul strolls the streets of Athens and observes the temples of the various gods he finds there. He reports that he "looked carefully" at the "objects of . . . worship" he found there (Acts 17:22), which he notes were "formed by the art and imagination" of the people (Acts 17:29). He read their literature, knew it well enough to quote, and treated it respectfully enough to incorporate it into his preaching about Christ. In fact, it even contains some of God's truth, Paul says, for he quotes it as saying, "As even some of your own poets have said, 'For we too are his offspring'" (Acts 17:28). A commitment to the radical transformation of society does not mean that Christians have to oppose everything about society. Society is not so much totally godless—"for in him we live and move and have our being"—as God-unaware.

In a similar way, we need to be observant in our workplaces. We can find many good practices in our schools, our businesses, in government, or other workplaces, even though they do not arise within the Christian community. If we are truly observant, we see that even those unaware or scornful of Christ are nonetheless made in the image of God. Like Paul, we should cooperate with them, rather than try to discredit them. We can work with nonbelievers to improve labor/management relationships, customer service, research and development, corporate and civic governance, public education, and other fields. We should make use of the skills and insights developed in universities, corporations, nonprofits, and other places. Our role is not to condemn their work, but to deepen it and show that it proves that "he is not far from each one of us" (Acts 17:27). Imagine the difference between saying, "Because you don't know Christ, all your work is wrong," and "Because I know Christ, I think I can appreciate your work even more than you do."

Yet at the same time, we need to be observant about the brokenness and sin evident in our workplaces. Our purpose is not to judge but to heal, or at least to limit the damage. Paul is particularly observant of the sin and distortion of idolatry. "He was deeply distressed to see that the city was full of idols" (Acts 17:16). The idols of modern workplaces, like the idols of ancient Athens, are many and varied. A Christian leader in New York City says,

> When I'm working with educators, whose idol is that all the world's problems will be solved by education, my heart connects to their heart about wanting to solve the world's problems, but I would point out to them that

they can only go so far with education, but the real solution comes from Christ. The same is true for many other professions.[20]

Our careful observations, like Paul's, make us more astute witnesses of Christ's unique power to set the world to rights.

> "While God has overlooked the times of human ignorance, now he commands all people everywhere to repent, because he has fixed a day on which he will have the world judged in righteousness by a man whom he has appointed, and of this he has given assurance to all by raising him from the dead." (Acts 17:30–31)

Tent-Making and Christian Life (Acts 18:1–4)

The passage most often connected to work in the book of Acts is Paul's tent-making in Acts 18:1–4. Although this passage is familiar, it is often understood too narrowly. In the familiar reading, Paul earns money by making tents, in order to support himself in his real ministry of witnessing to Christ. This view is too narrow, because it doesn't see that the tent-making itself is a real ministry of witnessing to Christ. Paul is a witness when he preaches and when he makes tents and uses his earnings to benefit the broader community.

This fits directly into Luke's view that the Spirit empowers Christians to use their resources for the sake of the whole community, which in turn witnesses to the gospel. Remember that Luke's orienting idea for Christian life is that of witness, and the entirety of one's life has the potential to bear witness. It is striking, then, that Paul is an exemplar of this Spirit-formed practice.

It is certainly true that Paul wants to support himself. Yet his impulse was not only to support himself in his preaching ministry, but also to provide financial support to the entire community. When Paul describes his economic impact among the Ephesians, he says:

> I coveted no one's silver or gold or apparel. You yourselves know that these hands ministered to my necessities, *and to those who were with*

---

[20] Telephone interview with Katherine Leary Alsdorf, Executive Director, Center for Faith and Work, Redeemer Presbyterian Church, New York, December 15, 2012.

me. In all things *I have shown you that by so toiling one must help the weak,* remembering the words of the Lord Jesus, how he said, *"It is more blessed to give than to receive."* (Acts 20:33–35, emphasis added, RSV)

Paul's money-earning work was an effort to build up the community economically.[21] Paul employs his skills and possessions for the sake of the community, and he explicitly says that this is an example others should follow. He does not say that everyone should follow his example of preaching. But he does say everyone should follow his example of toiling to help the weak and being generous in giving, as Jesus himself taught. Ben Witherington argues convincingly that Paul is not claiming any higher status arising from his apostolic position, but rather is "stepping down the social ladder for the sake of Christ."[22]

In other words, it is not the case that Paul engages in tent-making as a necessity so that he can do his "real job" of preaching. Instead, Paul's varieties of work in the sewing shop, marketplace, synagogue, lecture hall, and prison are all forms of witness. In any of these contexts, Paul participates in God's restorative project. In any of these contexts, Paul lives out his new identity in Christ for the sake of God's glory and out of love for his neighbors—even his former enemies. Even as he is being transported across the sea as a prisoner, he employs his gifts of leadership and encouragement to guide the soldiers and sailors holding him captive to safety during a severe storm (Acts 27:21–38). If he had not had the gift of being a preacher and apostle, he would still have been a witness to Christ simply by the way he engaged in making tents, toiling for the sake of the community, and working for the good of others in all situations.

"Tent-making" has become a common metaphor for Christians who engage in a money-earning profession as a means to support what is often called "professional ministry." The term "bi-vocational" is often used to indicate that two separate professions are involved, the money-earning one and the ministry one. But Paul's example shows that all aspects of human life should be a seamless witness. There is little room to draw

---

[21] This ethic is also expressed by Paul in 1 Thessalonians 1:9 and 1 Corinthians 9:1–15.

[22] Witherington, 547.

distinctions between "professional ministry" and other forms of witness. According to Acts, Christians actually have only one vocation—witnessing to the gospel. We have many forms of service, including preaching and pastoral care, making tents, building furniture, giving money, and caring for the weak. A Christian who engages in a money-earning profession such as making tents, in order to support a non-money-earning profession such as teaching about Jesus, would be more accurately described as "dual-service" rather than "bi-vocational"—one calling, two forms of service. The same would be true of any Christian who serves in more than one line of work.

The Gospel and Limits to Vocation and Engagement (Acts 19:17–20)

Acts 19:13–16 presents an odd story that leads to the repentance of "a number of those who had practiced magic" (Acts 19:19). They collected their magic books and burned them publicly, and Luke tells us that the value of the scrolls burned by these converts was 50,000 drachmas. This has been estimated as the equivalent to 137 years of continuous wages for a day laborer or enough bread to feed 100 families for 500 days.[23] Incorporation into the community of God's kingdom has massive economic and vocational impact.

While we cannot be certain whether those who repented of their engagement in magic were repenting of a means of earning a living, such a costly collection of books was unlikely to have been a mere hobby. Here we see that the change in life precipitated by faith in Jesus is immediately reflected in a vocational decision—a result familiar from Luke's Gospel. In this case, the believers found it necessary to abandon their former occupation entirely.

In many other cases, it is possible to remain in a vocation but necessary to practice it in a different way. For example, imagine that a salesperson has built a business selling unnecessary insurance to senior citizens. He or she would have to cease that practice, but could continue in the profession of selling insurance sales by switching to a product line that is beneficial for those who buy it. The commissions might be less (or

---

[23] Darrell L. Bock, *Acts*, Baker Exegetical Commentary on the New Testament (Grand Rapids: Baker, 2007), 605.

not), but the profession has plenty of room for legitimate success and lots of ethical participants.

A much more difficult situation occurs in professions that could be done legitimately, but in which illicit practices are so thoroughly entrenched that it is difficult to compete without violating biblical principles. Many civil servants in high-corruption nations face this dilemma. It might be possible to be an honest building inspector, but very difficult to do if your official pay is $10 a week and your supervisor demands a $100 a month fee to let you keep your job. A Christian in that situation faces a difficult choice. If all the honest people leave the profession, so much the worse for the public. But if it is difficult or impossible to make a living honestly in the profession, how can a Christian remain there? This is something Luke discusses in Luke 3:9, when John the Baptist counsels soldiers and tax collectors to remain in their jobs but to cease the extortion and fraud practiced by most of their profession. (See the section on Luke 3:1–14 in "Luke and Work" for more on this passage.)

Leadership as Witness (Acts 20–28)

The last eight chapters of Acts present an action-packed account of an attempt on Paul's life, followed by his imprisonment at the hands of two Roman governors and his harrowing shipboard journey to trial in Rome. In many ways, Paul's experience recapitulates the culmination of Jesus' ministry, and Acts 20–28 could be thought of as a kind of Passion of Paul. The aspect of these chapters most relevant to work is the depiction of Paul's leadership. We will focus on what we see of his courage, his suffering, his respect for others, and his concern for the well-being of others.

Paul's Courage

After the conflicts in Philippi and Ephesus, Paul receives threats of imprisonment (Acts 20:23; 21:11) and death (Acts 20:3; 23:12–14). These threats are not idle, for indeed two attempts are actually made on his life (Acts 21:31; 23:21). Paul is taken into custody by the Roman government (Acts 23:10) and a suit is brought against him (Acts 24:1–9), which, though false, ultimately leads to his execution. Given the episodes of conflict we have already explored, it is no surprise that following the ways of God's kingdom leads to conflict with the oppressive ways of the world.

Yet through it all, Paul maintains an extraordinary courage. He continues his work (preaching) despite the threats, and even dares to preach to his captors, both Jewish (Acts 23:1–10) and Roman (Acts 24:21–26; 26:32; 28:30–31). In the end, his courage proves decisive, not only for his work of preaching, but for saving the lives of hundreds of people in the midst of a shipwreck (Acts 27:22–23). His own words sum up his attitude of courage as those around him shrink back in fear. "What are you doing, weeping and breaking my heart? For I am ready not only to be bound but even to die in Jerusalem for the name of the Lord Jesus" (Acts 21:13).

The point, however, is not that Paul is a man of extraordinary courage, but that the Holy Spirit gives each of us the courage we need to do our work. Paul credits the Holy Spirit for keeping him going in the face of such adversity (Acts 20:22; 21:4; 23:11). This is an encouragement to us today, because we also can depend on the Holy Spirit to give us the courage we may lack. The danger is not so much that courage may fail us in the moment of greatest terror, but that general worry will deter us from taking even the first step into following the ways of God's kingdom in our work. How often do we fail to defend a colleague, serve a customer, challenge a boss, or speak up about an issue, not because we are under actual pressure, but because we are afraid that if we do we might offend someone in authority? What if we adopted a position that before we will act contrary to God's ways at work, we at least have to receive an actual order to do so? Could we begin by counting on the Holy Spirit to sustain us at least that far?

Paul's Suffering

Paul needs every ounce of courage because of the heavy sufferings he knows his work will bring. "The Holy Spirit testifies to me in every city that imprisonment and persecutions are waiting for me" (Acts 20:23), he says. He is kidnapped (Acts 21:27), beaten (Acts 21:30–31; 23:3), threatened (Acts 22:22; 27:42), arrested many times (Acts 21:33; 22:24, 31; 23:35; 28:16), accused in lawsuits (Acts 21:34; 22:30; 24:1–2; 25:2, 7; 28:4), interrogated (Acts 25:24–27), ridiculed (Acts 26:24), ignored (Acts 27:11), shipwrecked (Acts 27:41) and bitten by a viper (Acts 28:3). Tradition says that Paul is eventually put to death for his work, although this is not recounted anywhere in the Bible.

Leadership in a broken world entails suffering. Anyone who will not accept suffering as an essential element of leadership cannot be a leader, at least not a leader in the way God intends. In this, we see another radical refutation of the Roman patronage system. The Roman system is structured to insulate the patron from suffering. Patrons alone, for example, had the right to escape corporal punishment, as we see when Paul's status as a citizen (a patron, albeit of a household of one) is the only thing that protects him from an arbitrary flogging (Acts 22:29). Paul nonetheless embraces bodily suffering, along with many other forms, as the necessity of a leader in Jesus' way. Today, we may seek to become leaders for the same reason men in ancient Rome sought to exercise patronage—to avoid suffering. We might succeed in gaining power and perhaps even insulating ourselves from the hurts of the world. But our leadership cannot benefit others if we will not accept hurt to ourselves to a greater or lesser degree. And if our leadership does not benefit others, it is not God's kind of leadership.

Paul's Respect

Despite Paul's utter conviction that he is in the right about both his beliefs and his conduct, he shows respect for everyone he encounters. This is so disarming, especially to those who are his enemies and captors, that it gives him an unimpeachable opportunity as a witness of God's kingdom. When he arrives in Jerusalem, he respects the Jewish Christian leaders there and complies with their odd request to demonstrate his continued faithfulness to the Jewish law (Acts 21:17–26). He speaks respectfully to a crowd that has just beaten him (Acts 21:30–22:21), to a soldier who is about to flog him (Acts 22:25–29), to the Jewish council that accuses him in a Roman court of law—even to the point of apologizing for inadvertently insulting the high priest—(Acts 23:1–10), to the Roman governor Felix and his wife Drusilla (Acts 24:10–26), to Felix's successor Festus (Acts 25:8–11; 26:24–26), and to King Agrippa and his wife Bernice (Acts 26:2–29) who imprison him. On his journey there, he treats with respect the centurion Julius (Acts 27:3), the governor of Malta (Acts 28:7–10), and the leaders of the Jewish community in Rome (Acts 28:17–28).

We should not confuse the respect Paul shows with timidity about his message. Paul never shrinks from boldly proclaiming the truth, wherever the chips may fall. After being beaten by a Jewish crowd in Jerusalem who falsely suspect him of bringing a Gentile into the temple, he preaches a sermon to them that concludes with the Lord Jesus commissioning him to preach salvation to the Gentiles (Acts 22:17–21). He tells the Jewish council in Acts 23:1–8, "I am on trial concerning the hope of the resurrection of the dead" (Acts 23:6). He proclaims the gospel to Felix (Acts 24:14–16) and proclaims to Festus, Agrippa, and Bernice, "I stand here on trial on account of my hope in the promise made by God to our ancestors" (Acts 26:6). He warns the soldiers and sailors on the boat to Rome that "the voyage will be with danger and much heavy loss, not only of the cargo and the ship, but also of our lives" (Acts 27:10). The book of Acts ends with Paul "proclaiming the kingdom of God and teaching about the Lord Jesus Christ with all boldness and without hindrance" (Acts 28:30–31).

Paul's respect for others often wins him a hearing and even turns enemies into friends, notwithstanding the boldness of his words. The centurion about to flog him intervenes with the Roman tribune, who orders him released (Acts 22:26–29). The Pharisees conclude, "We find nothing wrong with this man. What if a spirit or an angel has spoken to him?" (Acts 23:9). Felix determines that Paul "was charged with nothing deserving death or imprisonment" (Acts 23:29) and becomes an avid listener who "used to send for him very often and converse with him" (Acts 24:26). Agrippa, Bernice, and Festus come to see that Paul is innocent, and Agrippa begins to be persuaded by Paul's preaching. "Are you so quickly persuading me to become a Christian?" he asks (Acts 26:28). By the end of the voyage to Rome, Paul has become the de facto leader of the ship, issuing orders that the captain and centurion are happy to obey (Acts 27:42–44). On Malta, the governor welcomes and entertains Paul and his companions, and later provisions their ship and sends them away with honor (Acts 28:10).

Not everyone returns Paul's respect with respect, of course. Some vilify, reject, threaten, and abuse him. But, in general, he receives far more respect from people than do the masters of the Roman patronage system among whom he operates. The exercise of power may command the appearance of respect, but the exercise of true respect is much more likely to earn a response of true respect.

Paul's Concern for Others

Most of all, Paul's leadership is marked by his concern for others. He accepts the burden of leadership not to make his life better, but to make others' lives better. His very willingness to travel to hostile places to preach a better way of life is proof enough of this. Yet we also see his concern for others in concrete, personal ways. He heals a boy who is severely injured by a fall from an upper-floor window (Acts 20:9–12). He prepares the churches he has planted to carry on after his death, and encourages them when they are overcome with "much weeping" (Acts 20:37). He attempts to preach the good news even to those who are trying to kill him (Acts 22:1–21). He heals all the sick on the island of Malta (Acts 28:8–10).

A striking example of his concern for others occurs during the shipwreck. Although his warning not to make the voyage had been ignored, Paul pitches in to help and encourage the crew and passengers when the storm strikes.

> Since they had been without food for a long time, Paul then stood up among them and said, "Men, you should have listened to me and not have set sail from Crete and thereby avoided this damage and loss. I urge you now to keep up your courage, for there will be no loss of life among you, but only of the ship. For last night there stood by me an angel of the God to whom I belong and whom I worship, and he said, 'Do not be afraid, Paul; you must stand before the emperor; and indeed, God has granted safety to all those who are sailing with you.' So keep up your courage, men, for I have faith in God that it will be exactly as I have been told." (Acts 27:21–25)

His concern does not end with words of encouragement but proceeds with practical acts. He makes sure everyone eats to keep up their strength (Acts 27:34–36). He devises a plan that will save everyone's life, including those who can't swim (Acts 27:26, 38, 41, 44). He directs preparations for running the ship aground (Acts 27:43b), and prevents the sailors from abandoning the soldiers and passengers (Acts 27:30–32). As a result of his concerns and actions, not a single life is lost in the wreck (Acts 27:44).

Paul's leadership encompasses far more than the four factors of courage, suffering, respect, and concern for others, and it is visible far beyond Acts 20–28. Yet these factors as presented in these chapters form one of the most stirring demonstrations of leadership in the Bible and remain as much of an example today as they were in Luke's day.

Conclusion to Acts

Investigating work and work-related issues in Acts presents a coherent treatment of vocation in God's world. In Acts, a Christian view of work is not relegated simply to the realm of ethics. Rather, work is an active form of witness in God's redemption of the world. The logic of Acts moves in this direction:

1. The coming of the Spirit initiates Christ's kingdom—God's new world—in a new way. The Roman patronage system that seeks status for the self is replaced with a spirit of love that seeks the good of others. This follows the example of Jesus who spends himself for the sake of others—evident above all in the cross.

2. The Christian vocation is characterized by Spirit-empowered witness to Christ's kingdom, not only by proclamation but also by acting in accord with God's spirit of love in everyday life.

3. The Christian vocation is given to the entire community of believers, not merely to individuals. The believers' practice is not perfect—sometimes very far from perfect—but it is a real participation in the new world, nonetheless.

4. The community bears witness to Christ's kingdom by working and using work-related resources—power, wealth, and status—for the sake of others and the community as a whole. Membership in the community goes hand in hand with a transformed way of life, leading to love and service. An exemplary result is the practice of radical generosity with every kind of resource.

5. When work is performed in this way, every profession can be an act of witness by practicing the structures of justice, righteousness, and beauty brought forth by God's kingdom.

6. The Christian community thus produces a way of working that challenges the structures of the fallen world, and sometimes brings it into conflict with the world's power-holders. Nonetheless, the intent of the community is not to clash with the world but to transform it.

7. Leadership is a prominent arena in which the new spirit of love and service for others is enacted. Authority is shared and leadership is encouraged at every level of the community. Leaders accept the burden of acting for the good of others, and they respect the wisdom and authority of those they lead. Leadership attributes—including courage, suffering, respect, and concern for others—come to the fore in the example of the Apostle Paul.

Acts helps us to see that all of human life—including our work and the fruit that emerges from our work—can be a means of participating through the power of the Spirit already emerging in God's kingdom coming to earth. In this way work is not only dignified but also essential to the human vocation of witness. As it was from the beginning, work is central to what it means to be fully human. Workers today are called to be cultivators and transformers of earth, culture, family, business, education, justice, and every other sphere—all for the sake of God's kingdom.

Bibliography

Albright, W. F., and C. S. Mann. *Matthew*. Vol. 26, *The Anchor Bible*. New York: Doubleday, 1971.

Barclay, William. *The Gospel of Matthew*. Louisville, KY: Westminster John Knox Press, 2001.

Bartchy, S. Scott. "Community of Goods in Acts: Idealization or Social Reality?" In *The Future of Early Christianity: Essays in Honor of Helmut Koester*. Edited by Birger A. Pearson, A. Thomas Krabel, George W. E. Nickelsburg, and Norman R. Petersen. Minneapolis: Fortress Press, 1991.

Bauckham, Richard J. *God Crucified: Monotheism and Christology in the New Testament*. Grand Rapids: Eerdmans, 1999.

———. "Jesus' Demonstration in the Temple." In *Law and Religion: Essays on the Place of the Law in Israel and Early Christianity*. Edited by B. Lindars, 72–89. Cambridge: James Clarke, 1988.

Bock, Darrell L. *Acts. Baker Exegetical Commentary on the New Testament*. Grand Rapids: Baker, 2007.

———. *Luke 9:51–24:53. Baker Exegetical Commentary on the New Testament*. Grand Rapids: Baker Books, 1996.

Bruner, Frederick Dale. *The Christbook, Matthew 1–12*. Vol. 1, *Matthew: A Commentary*. Grand Rapids: Wm. B. Eerdmans, 2007.

Byrne, Brendan. *The Hospitality of God: A Reading of Luke's Gospel*. Collegeville, MN: Liturgical Press, 2000.

Campbell, Ken M. "What was Jesus' Occupation?" *Journal of the Evangelical Theological Society* 48, no. 3 (September 2005): 501–19.

Capper, Brian J. "The Interpretation of Acts 5.4." *Journal for the Study of the New Testament* 6, no. 19 (1983): 117–31.

———. "The Palestinian Cultural Context of Earliest Christian Community of Goods." In *The Book of Acts in Its Palestinian Setting*. Edited by Richard J. Bauckham, 323–56. Grand Rapids: Eerdmans, 1995.

Carson, D. A. *The Gospel According to John. The Pillar New Testament Commentary*. Grand Rapids: Eerdmans, 1991.

Cho, Youngmo. *Spirit and Kingdom in the Writings of Luke and Paul*. Waynesborough, GA: Paternoster, 2005.

Collins, Jim. *Good to Great: Why Some Companies Make the Leap . . . And Others Don't*. New York: HarperBusiness, 2001.

De Pree, Max. *Leadership Is an Art*. New York: Doubleday, 1989.

Doering, Lutz. "Sabbath Laws in the New Testament Gospels." In *The New Testament and Rabbinic Literature*. Edited by F. García Martínez and P. J. Tomson, 208–20. Leiden: Brill, 2009.

"Dr. Gary Kaplan: Determined Steps to Transformation." *Ethix* 73 (Jan. 2001). http://ethix.org/2011/01/11/dr-gary-s-kaplan-determined-steps-to-transformation.

Dunn, James D. G. *Acts of the Apostles. Epworth Commentaries*. Peterborough, UK: Epworth Press, 1996.

Evans, Craig A. "Jesus' Action in the Temple." In *Jesus in Context: Temple, Purity, and Restoration*. Edited by Craig A. Evans and B. Chilton, 395–44. Leiden: Brill, 1997.

Fitzmyer, Joseph A. *The Acts of the Apostles. The Anchor Bible*. New York: Doubleday, 1998.

France, R. T. *The Gospel of Matthew. New International Commentary on the New Testament*. Grand Rapids: Eerdmans, 2007.

Freedman, David Noel. *The Anchor Yale Bible Dictionary*. Vol. 5. New York: Doubleday, 1996.

Freyne, Sean. *Jesus: A Jewish Galilean*. London: T&T Clark, 2004.

Frost, Robert. "The Tuft of Flowers." In *A Boy's Will*. New York: Henry Holt, 1915.

Gill, David. *Becoming Good: Building Moral Character*. Downers Grove: InterVarsity Press, 2000.

Greenleaf, Robert. *Servant Leadership*. Mahwah, NJ: Paulist Press, 1977.

Greer, Peter, and Phil Smith. *The Poor Will Be Glad*. Grand Rapids: Zondervan, 2009.

Guelich, Robert A. *Mark 1–8:26*. Vol. 34A, *Word Biblical Commentary*. Nashville: Thomas Nelson, 1989.

Hagner, Donald A. *Matthew 1–13*. Vol. 33A, *Word Biblical Commentary*. Nashville: Thomas Nelson, 1993.

———. *Matthew 14–18*. Vol. 33B, *Word Biblical Commentary*. Nashville: Thomas Nelson, 1995.

Harland, Philip A. *Associations, Synagogues, and Congregations: Creating a Place in Ancient Mediterranean Society*. Minneapolis: Augsburg Fortress, 2003.

Hauerwas, Stanley, and William Willimon. *Resident Aliens: Life in the Christian Colony*. Nashville: Abingdon Press, 1989.

Hays, Christopher M. *Luke's Wealth Ethics: A Study in Their Coherence and Character*. Wissenschaftliche Untersuchungen zum Neuen Testament 2.275. Tubingen: Mohr-Siebeck, 2010.

Henderson, Suzanne Watts. *Christology and Discipleship in the Gospel of Mark*. Cambridge: Cambridge University Press, 2006.

Hester, J. David. "Dramatic Inconclusion: Irony and the Narrative Rhetoric of the Ending of Mark." *Journal for the Study of the New Testament* 17 (1995): 61–86.

Huggett, Joyce. *Finding God in the Fast Lane*. Suffolk, UK: Kevin Mayhew, 2004.

Kaiser, Jr., Walter C., and Duane Garrett, editors. *Archaeological Study Bible*. Grand Rapids: Zondervan, 2006.

Karass, Chester L. *In Business and in Life: You Don't Get What You Deserve, You Get What You Negotiate*. N.p.: Stanford Street Press, 1996.

"Kendrick B. Melrose: Caring about People: Employees and Customers." *Ethix* 55 (Sept. 2007). http://ethix.org/2007/10/01/caring-about-people-employees-and-customers.

Klawans, J. *Purity, Sacrifice, and the Temple: Symbolism and Supersessionism in the Study of Ancient Judaism*. New York: Oxford University Press, 2005.

Kloppenborg, John S. "Collegia and *Thiasoi*: Issues in Function, Taxonomy and Membership." In *Voluntary Associations in the Graeco-Roman World*. Edited by John S. Kloppenborg and S. G. Wilson, 16–30. London: Routledge, 1996.

Kuecker, Aaron J. "The Spirit and the 'Other,' Satan and the 'Self': Economic Ethics as a Consequence of Identity Transformation in Luke-Acts." In *Engaging Economics: New Testament Scenarios and Early Christian Reception*. Edited by Bruce W. Longenecker and Kelly D. Liebengood, 81–103. Grand Rapids: Eerdmans, 2009.

Levison, John R. *Filled with the Spirit*. Grand Rapids: Eerdmans, 2009.

Lienhard, Joseph T. "Acts 6.1–6: A Redactional View." *Catholic Biblical Quarterly* 37 (1975): 232.

Malina, Bruce, and Richard Rohrbaugh. *A Social-Scientific Commentary on the Synoptic Gospels*. Minneapolis: Fortress, 1992.

Melrose, Ken. Correspondence to the Theology of Work Project. July 30, 2013.

Mitchell, Alan C. "The Social Function of Friendship in Acts 2.44–47 and 4.32–37." *Journal of Biblical Literature* 111, no. 2 (1992).

Moltmann, Jürgen. *The Way of Jesus Christ*. Minneapolis: Fortress Press, 1995.

Nolland, John. *Luke 1–9:20*. Vol. 35A, *Word Biblical Commentary*. Nashville: Thomas Nelson, 1989.

Pao, David W. *Acts and the Isaianic New Exodus*. Grand Rapids: Baker Academic, 2002.

Penney, John Michael. "The Missionary Emphasis of Lukan Pneumatology." *Journal of Pentecostal Theology*. Sheffield, UK: Sheffield Academic Press, 1997.

Peters, Tom. *Thriving on Chaos*. New York: Knopf, 1987.

Richardson, Alan. *The Biblical Doctrine of Work. Ecumenical Bible Studies no. 1*. London: SCM Press for the Study Department of the World Council of Churches, 1952. Reprinted 1954.

Sanders, E. P. *Jesus and Judaism*. Philadelphia: Fortress Press, 1985.

Shepherd, David. *Seeking Sabbath: A Personal Journey*. Oxford: Bible Reading Fellowship, 2007.

Stein, Robert H. *Luke*. Nashville: Broadman, 1992.

Sterling, Gregory E. "'Athletes of Virtue': An Analysis of the Summaries in Acts (2.41–47; 4.32–35; 5.12–16)." *Journal of Biblical Literature* 113, no. 4 (1994).

Strom, Stephanie. "Pledge to Give Away Half Gains Billionaire Adherents." *New York Times*, August 4, 2010.

Terkel, Studs. *Working*. New York: The New Press, 1972.

Tiede, David L. "The Exaltation of Jesus and the Restoration of Israel in Acts 1." *Harvard Theological Review* 79, no. 1 (1986).

Willard, Dallas. *The Spirit of the Disciplines: Understanding How God Changes Lives*. San Francisco: Harper and Row, 1988.

Witherington III, Ben. *The Acts of the Apostles: A Socio-Rhetorical Commentary*. Grand Rapids: Eerdmans, 1998.

Wright, N. T. *Jesus and the Victory of God*. London: SPCK, 1996.

Contributors

John Alsdorf resides in New York City and is a member of the Theology of Work Project's steering committee.

Katherine Leary Alsdorf is founder and director emeritus of the Center for Faith and Work at Redeemer Presbyterian Church in New York City. She is a member of the Theology of Work Project's steering committee.

Patricia Anders is editorial director of Hendrickson Publishers in Peabody, Massachusetts. She serves as editorial director for the commentary.

Jill L. Baker is an independent researcher of ancient Near Eastern archaeology and faculty fellow at Florida International University, Honors College, in Miami, Florida. She contributed to the commentary on 1 and 2 Samuel, 1 and 2 Kings, and 1 and 2 Chronicles.

Cara Beed is retired lecturer in sociology in the Department of Social Science, retired graduate advisor for the Faculty of Education, and retired honorary fellow at the Australian Catholic University in Melbourne, Victoria, Australia. She is a writer and researcher with works published in many international journals. She is a member of the Theology of Work Project's steering committee.

Daniel Block is the Gunther H. Knoedler Professor of Old Testament at Wheaton College in Wheaton, Illinois. He contributed to the commentary on Ruth.

Daniel T. Byrd is special assistant to the provost at the University of La Verne in La Verne, California. He served as a member of the Theology of Work Project's steering committee from 2007 to 2009.

Alice Camille is a nationally known Roman Catholic author, religious educator, and retreat leader. She resides in Desert Hot Springs, California. She contributed to the commentary on Joshua and Judges.

Darrell Cosden is professor of theological studies at Judson University in Elgin, Illinois. He served as a member of the Theology of Work Project's steering committee from 2007 to 2010.

Al Erisman is executive in residence at Seattle Pacific University in Seattle, Washington, and former director of technology at the Boeing Company. He serves as co-chair of the Theology of Work Project's steering committee. He contributed to the commentary on 2 John and 3 John.

Nancy S. Erisman volunteers as a board member of KIROS and on the leadership team at Westminster Chapel Women in the Workplace in Bellevue, Washington. She served as a contributing editor to the commentary.

Jarrett Fontenot resides in Baton Rouge, Louisiana. He served as a contributing editor to the commentary.

Larry Fowler resides in Gig Harbor, Washington. He served as a contributing editor to the commentary.

Russell Fuller is professor of Old Testament at Southern Baptist Theological Seminary in Louisville, Kentucky. He contributed to the commentary on Psalms.

Duane A. Garrett is the John R. Sampey Professor of Old Testament Interpretation at Southern Baptist Theological Seminary in Louisville, Kentucky. He contributed to the commentary on Deuteronomy, Ecclesiastes, and Song of Songs, and served as editor for the poetical books.

Mark S. Gignilliat is associate professor of divinity at Beeson Divinity School, Samford University in Birmingham, Alabama. He contributed to the commentary on Isaiah and served as editor for the prophetic books.

Michaiah Healy is youth pastor at the Greater Boston Vineyard in Cambridge, Massachusetts. She served as a contributing editor to the commentary.

Bill Heatley is the former executive director of Dallas Willard Ministries in Oak Park, California, and served as a member of the Theology of Work Project's steering committee from 2007 to 2014. He contributed to the commentary on Colossians and Philemon.

Bill Hendricks is president of the Giftedness Center in Dallas, Texas. He is a member of the Theology of Work Project's steering committee.

Brian Housman is executive pastor at the Vineyard Christian Fellowship of Greater Boston in Cambridge, Massachusetts. He contributed to the commentary on 1 and 2 Samuel, 1 and 2 Kings, and 1 and 2 Chronicles.

L. T. Jeyachandran is former chief engineer (civil) at the Department of Telecommunications for the government of India in Calcutta, India, and former executive director of Ravi Zacharias International Ministries (Asia-Pacific) in Singapore. He is a member of the Theology of Work Project's steering committee.

Timothy Johnson is assistant professor of Old Testament and Hebrew at Nashotah House Theological Seminary in Nashotah, Wisconsin. He contributed to the commentary on Job.

Randy Kilgore is senior writer and workplace chaplain at Desired Haven Ministries/Made to Matter in North Beverly, Massachusetts. He is a member of the Theology of Work Project's steering committee.

Alexander N. Kirk resides in Wilmington, Delaware, and contributed to the commentary on 1 and 2 Timothy and Titus.

Aaron Kuecker is associate professor of theology and director of the Honors College at LeTourneau University in Longview, Texas. He contributed to the commentary on Luke and Acts.

Jon C. Laansma is associate professor of classical languages and New Testament at Wheaton College and Wheaton Graduate School in Wheaton, Illinois. He contributed to the commentary on Hebrews.

Clint Le Bruyns is director and senior lecturer at the Theology and Development Programme at the University of KwaZulu-Natal in Pietermaritzburg, KwaZulu-Natal, South Africa. He is a member of the Theology of Work Project's steering committee.

John G. Lewis is director of Saint Benedict's Workshop and Missioner for Christian Formation at the Episcopal Diocese of West Texas in San Antonio, Texas. He consulted on the commentary on Romans.

Kelly Liebengood is associate professor of biblical studies at LeTourneau University in Longview, Texas. He contributed to the commentary on James, 1 and 2 Peter, 1 John, and Jude.

Kerry E. Luddy is director of community relations and discipleship at Brighton Presbyterian Church in Rochester, New York. She served as a contributing editor to the commentary.

Grant Macaskill is senior lecturer in New Testament studies at the University of Saint Andrews in St. Andrews, Fife, Scotland, United Kingdom. He contributed to the commentary on Mark.

Alistair Mackenzie is senior lecturer at the School of Theology, Mission and Ministry, Laidlaw College in Christchurch, New Zealand. He is a member of the Theology of Work Project's steering committee.

Ryan P. Marshall is minister to students at Redeemer Community Church in Needham, Massachusetts. He served as a contributing editor to the commentary.

Steven D. Mason is associate provost and dean of faculty at LeTourneau University in Longview, Texas. He contributed to the commentary on Ezekiel.

Alice Mathews is the Lois W. Bennett Distinguished Professor Emerita at Gordon-Conwell Theological Seminary in South Hamilton, Massachusetts. She is a member of the Theology of Work Project's steering committee. She contributed to the commentary on Genesis 1–11, Proverbs, 1 and 2 Samuel, 1 and 2 Kings, 1 and 2 Chronicles, Introduction to the Prophets, Isaiah, Jeremiah, Lamentations, and Matthew. She also served as a consulting editor for the commentary.

Kenneth Mathews is professor of divinity at Beeson Divinity School, Samford University, in Birmingham, Alabama. He contributed to the commentary on Daniel.

Sean McDonough is professor of New Testament at Gordon-Conwell Theological Seminary in South Hamilton, Massachusetts. He is a member of the Theology of Work Project's steering committee. He contributed to the commentary on Joshua, Judges, John, and Revelation, and served as editor for biblical studies and the Epistles.

Tim Meadowcroft is senior lecturer in biblical studies at Laidlaw College in Auckland, New Zealand. He contributed to the commentary on Hosea, Joel, Amos, Obadiah, Micah, Nahum, Habakkuk, Zephaniah, Haggai, Zechariah, and Malachi.

William Messenger is executive editor of the Theology of Work Project in Boston, Massachusetts, and adjunct faculty member of

Laidlaw-Carey Graduate School in Auckland, New Zealand. He also serves on the board of directors of ArQule, Inc. He is a member of the Theology of Work Project's steering committee. He contributed to the commentary on Jonah and served as general editor.

Andy Mills is former president and CEO at Thomson Financial and Professional Publishing Group in Boston, Massachusetts. He serves as co-chair of the Theology of Work Project's steering committee.

Joshua Moon resides in Minneapolis, Minnesota. He contributed to the commentary on Jeremiah and Lamentations.

Colin R. Nicholl is an independent researcher and author in Northern Ireland, United Kingdom. He contributed to the commentary on 1 and 2 Thessalonians.

Valerie O'Connell is an independent consultant in Burlington, Massachusetts. She served as a contributing editor to the commentary.

Jane Lancaster Patterson is assistant professor of New Testament at Seminary of the Southwest in Austin, Texas. She consulted on the commentary on Romans.

Jonathan T. Pennington is associate professor of New Testament and director of PhD studies at Southern Baptist Theological Seminary in Louisville, Kentucky. He contributed to the commentary on Matthew and served as editor for the Gospels and Acts.

Gordon Preece is director of Ethos: the Evangelical Alliance Centre for Christianity and Society in Melbourne, Victoria, Australia. He is a member of the Theology of Work Project's steering committee.

Mark D. Roberts is executive director of digital media at the H. E. Butt Family Foundation/The High Calling in Kerrville, Texas. He is a member of the Theology of Work Project's steering committee. He contributed to the commentary on Ezra, Nehemiah, Esther, Galatians, Ephesians, and Philippians.

Haddon Robinson is the Harold John Ockenga Distinguished Professor of Preaching, senior director of the Doctor of Ministry program, and former interim president of Gordon-Conwell Theological Seminary in South Hamilton, Massachusetts. He is president and chair emeritus of the Theology of Work Project.

Justin Schell is on the global leadership and support team with The Lausanne Movement. He served as a contributing editor to the commentary.

Andrew J. Schmutzer is professor of biblical studies at Moody Bible Institute in Chicago, Illinois. He contributed to the commentary on Genesis 1–11.

Bob Stallman is professor of Bible and Hebrew at Northwest University in Kirkland, Washington. He contributed to the commentary on Genesis 12–50, Exodus, Leviticus, and Numbers.

Christine S. Tan is director of marketing and social media at the Theology of Work Project in Boston, Massachusetts. She served as a contributing editor to the commentary.

Hanno van der Bijl resides in Mobile, Alabama. He is web editor at the Theology of Work Project and served as a contributing editor to the commentary.

Bruce Waltke is professor emeritus of biblical studies at Regent College in Vancouver, British Columbia, Canada. He has also held teaching positions at Westminster Theological Seminary in Glenside, Pennsylvania, and Knox Theological Seminary in Fort Lauderdale, Florida, where he is a distinguished professor of Old Testament. He contributed to the commentary on Proverbs and served as editor for the Pentateuch.

Joel White is lecturer in New Testament at Giessen School of Theology in Giessen, Germany. He contributed to the commentary on 1 and 2 Corinthians.

Andy Williams is program manager at HOPE International in Kigali, Rwanda. He served as a contributing editor to the commentary.

David Williamson is director emeritus of Laity Lodge in Kerrville, Texas. He is a member of the Theology of Work Project's steering committee.

Lindsay Wilson is academic dean and senior lecturer in Old Testament at Ridley Melbourne Mission and Ministry College in Melbourne, Victoria, Australia. He contributed to the commentary on Psalms.

Index of Names and Subjects

Note: page numbers in *italics* indicate most significant occurrences.

About the Theology of Work Project

The Theology of Work Project is an independent, international organization dedicated to researching, writing, and distributing materials with a biblical perspective on work. The Project's primary mission is to produce resources covering every book of the Bible plus major topics in today's workplaces. Wherever possible, the Project collaborates with other faith-and-work organizations, churches, universities and seminaries to help equip people for meaningful, productive work of every kind.

Theology of Work Bible Commentary
By the Theology of Work Project

William Messenger, Executive Editor, Theology of Work Project
Sean McDonough, Biblical Editor, Theology of Work Project
Patricia Anders, Editorial Director, Hendrickson Publishers

Contributors to Volume 4:

Jonathan Pennington and Alice Mathews, "Matthew and Work"
Grant Macaskill, "Mark and Work"
Aaron Kuecker, "Luke and Work" and "Acts and Work"
Sean McDonough, "John and Work"